Good Housekeeping

THE ECOFRIENDLY HOME

Good Housekeeping

THE ECOFRIENDLY HOME

FRESH IDEAS FOR A HEALTHY HOME

DAN PHILLIPS

HarperCollins*Illustrated*

First published in 2000 by
HarperCollins*Illustrated*
an imprint of HarperCollins*Publishers*
77-85 Fulham Palace Road
London W6 8JB

The HarperCollins website address is:
www.**fire**and**water**.com

Published in association with
The National Magazine Company Limited.
Good Housekeeping is a registered
trade mark of
The National Magazine Company Limited
and the Hearst Corporation.

Text © 2000 Dan Phillips
Compilation © 2000 Carroll & Brown Limited

A cip catalogue record for this book is
available from the British Library.

ISBN 0-00-710073-6

This book was conceived, designed and
produced by
Carroll & Brown Limited
20 Lonsdale Road
London NW6 6RD

Colour reproduction by Colourscan
Printed and bound in Spain by Mondadori
with paper sourced from sustainable forests
D.L. TO: 1428 - 2000

This book is typeset in Rotis

Contents

1 **Eco-principles** 6

Why ecofriendly? 8
The key concepts 10

2 **Essential elements** 16

Surveying your home 18
Making space 20
Letting the light in 25
Encouraging clean air 29
Conserving water 33
Heating your home 37
Keeping cool 43
Colour, texture and pattern 46

3 **Eco-materials** 50

What makes an
eco-material? 52
Floor foundations 54
Floor coverings 56
Internal walls 65
External materials 71
Furnishings and fittings 74
Fabrics and fillings 80

4 **Rooms for living** 84

Entrances, halls and
stairs 86
Living rooms and lounging 90
Kitchens and cooking 96
Dining rooms and eating 104
Bedrooms and sleeping 108
Bathrooms and bathing 114
Studies and home working 124
Studios and bedsits 128

Basement living 130
Attics 132
Conservatories 134

5 **People and pets** 136

Babies 138
Children 142
Teenagers 146
Young adults 147
Later life 148
Pets 150
Allergies 152

6 **Upkeep** 154

Maintenance and repair 156
Household cleaning 161
Cleaning products 164
Waste management 168
Household pests 170

7 **Eco-rating guide** 172

Useful contact details 184
Index 186
Picture credits 190
Suppliers and
acknowledgements 191

Eco-principles

Many ecological home design books recommend that the only way forward is to move out of the city and build a self-sufficient retreat away from the madding crowd. No matter how appealing this idea may seem, few of us have the desire or the practical ability to start again. The reality is that urban living is here to stay, so we should all try to discover how we can move towards a more ecologically sympathetic and caring home life wherever it is we live.

Why ecofriendly?

Our homes protect us from the weather and provide us with a space where good memories and experiences grow. With a little extra thought on our part, they can also connect us with the pleasures of the natural world, keeping us in touch with the seasons and providing our families with a buffer against some of the frustrations of our fast and modern lives. Our homes also reflect ourselves, so it's equally important that we find a way of living which is comfortable and compatible with our personal outlook on life.

But why choose ecofriendly alternatives when you can surely do all these things without worrying too much about the consequences? The reasons are simple enough: ecofriendly homes are cleaner, more cost-effective and more fun. They use less, do more, last longer, support your local community and help you to connect with the outside world.

On a broader level, we are now faced with the need to improve the quality of our home environment, perhaps more so than any other time in our history. In the past 200 years, the world's population has increased from one billion to six billion, and we have changed from being a mainly pastoral and sedentary species into fast-living urban dwellers who travel frequently – and often globally.

We also consume vast quantities of fuel and materials, creating pollution and waste on an unprecedented scale.

Our homes, innocent though they may seem, are responsible for over half of all this consumption and also harbour the causes of many modern ailments. These are two clear reasons why we need to consider carefully the choices we make for our home.

WHAT MAKES AN ECOFRIENDLY HOME?

Ecology is the study of how living creatures interact with each other and the natural world, while

< express yourself
Your home should reflect your personality, so don't restrict your individual style – anything from kitsch to classic can be considered ecofriendly. Aim to strike a balance so that you can enjoy your immediate surroundings, and care for the long term as well.

More specifically, an ecofriendly home is one that is made from non-toxic materials that are easy to reuse or recycle; contains long-lasting, well-made and multifunctional furniture and fittings; uses energy thoughtfully so that it is efficient and cheap to run; is designed with the natural elements in mind so its interiors are connected with the outside, natural world; blends in well to be a part of your local community; and finally, has a sense of fun and comfort to it.

Instead of simply being 'a machine for living', try to make your home funky and tough. Break down the barriers between rooms, understand the surfaces and furniture in your home and enjoy them. Choose items that are multifunctional and adaptable: a table on wheels that splits in two can be used for writing, dining and even a play thing for the kids. A child's cot can turn into a chair and a climbing frame. As well as being comfortable and attractive, every item in an ecofriendly home should work and play hard too.

But do we have to live like eco-warriors to be ecofriendly? Of course not! Simple measures, such as changing a standard light bulb to a fluorescent one will make the lighting in your home last ten times longer. Switching to gas heating instead of electric will cut your energy bills, while fitting proper controls and insulating your windows will further reduce your home's energy consumption. Choosing wood flooring instead of fitted carpets will not only reduce your house cleaning work but will also make your floor last a lifetime. All it takes is a little knowledge and forethought.

∧ hardworking homes
Our homes should be flexible and fun, inspiring us to enjoy the world around us and able to adapt to our constantly changing needs. They should provide a calming environment in which we can either relax and be alone, or entertain and be sociable. Our homes should protect us against the elements and pollution of all kinds, and yet connect us with the world outside.

friendliness is a state of mind that puts care and good humour at the top of our agenda. Ecofriendly homes can therefore be defined as homes that are kind to the environment, to our families and to the people around us, both around the corner and around the rest of the globe.

The key concepts

Ecofriendly living encapsulates both basic and eclectic ideas. Some, such as recycling, are familiar and frequently practised in many homes. Others, such as choosing renewable sources of energy, may be less common. To start with, adopt the ones that suit you most, then explore the others as time goes by.

SUPPORT YOUR LOCAL COMMUNITY

No one is an island and the choices we make all have an effect on others and the planet. Being aware of this will help us to ensure that our actions help rather than harm. One way to do this is by finding local people to maintain your home and choosing locally-made products to furnish it. This benefits everyone by keeping cash in your community and providing common ground. It also avoids the transportation costs, energy and pollution which result from buying from afar. If you do buy products from distant communities, always pay a fair price for fair trade. Never buy products that have been made on the back of someone else's poverty. As the saying goes, 'think global, but act local'.

Think about ways of improving your community too. A tree-lined street with clean pavements and local shops will improve the quality of your life and add value to your home. Instead of complaining, think of ways to make your neighbourhood a cleaner, friendlier and safer place. Petition your council to slow down traffic, hold a fête in the street to raise money for local kids or even invite your neighbours for a picnic in the local park!

∧ **fresh and local**
Using your local greengrocer or market place in preference to out-of-town shopping centres will not only keep cash in your community, but will also help to improve the quality of your local neighbourhood.

SMALL IS BEAUTIFUL

Living simply often means doing more with less. Big and unwieldy homes are a bit like large, high-powered cars. They are invariably far harder to look after than smaller versions. Just like the mini-moke or the Fiat 500, smaller homes are easier to handle and personalise. But choosing small things doesn't mean rejecting quality. Like a vase or a handcrafted sculpture, a small home can be an object of beauty too. As the German-born architect Mies van der Rohe said, 'God is in the detail.'

RENEWABLE POWER

Of all the choices that we can make, the key to conserving resources is to find ways of making power stations and diesel-spewing trucks vanish. When you take out a normal light bulb and replace it with a compact fluorescent one, you remove the need to make 80 per cent of electricity and a power station will eventually disappear. When you replace a south-facing single-glazed window with a high-efficiency double glazed unit, the window captures more heat from the sun than it loses, becoming a natural heater. When you buy a second-hand mahogany table from the corner shop or hand one down to your children, a tree in Malaysia will not be chopped down, a forest may not be destroyed, a truck will not cross the country and a motorway may not be built.

Conserving energy and using renewable power needn't be a chore or a burden. In the not too distant future, we may all be installing our own mini power stations in our homes or local communities. Many experts predict that we will be purchasing micro fuel cells that can generate electricity by chemical reaction. These will run on ethanol (which is produced by growing crops like sugar cane) and their only waste product will be water.

Until this happens, there are plenty of other renewable energy technologies which use the sun or the wind to harness natural energy sources. The simplest and most widely available renewable energy is wood. Trees also absorb carbon dioxide and air pollution, and help to improve the quality of cities and the countryside. Growing trees is therefore a small but important part of sustainable living.

Photovoltaic systems are now available which can make any

alternative energy
Wind turbines (below) and solar photovoltaic tiles (right) are just two forms of renewable power now available. Even using sunshine instead of artificial lighting will encourage environmental protection.

existing home into a net exporter of electricity. Whilst uncommon and still expensive, it is likely that prices will fall and numbers will increase as manufacturers develop the technology.

Wind turbines are a common sight in windy rural locations where the cost of installing electrical cables or an oil-fired generator are high. Economies of scale suggest wind turbines will

ECOTIP

Ecofriendly electricity
Your home's electrical supply comes from a power station far away and it's easy to think that you can't control the way a supplier maintains their plant and how that affects your environment. Yet it is possible to choose your electricity from a company that delivers renewable electricity direct to your home. This reduces the need for companies to build new power stations, as well as pollution caused by the burning of fossil fuels. Future changes in technology will make even greater energy savings as lights and appliances will only turn on when they are needed and turn off automatically when you leave the room. Until then, do the planet a favour and switch off lights and heaters when they're not really needed.

probably develop into a major source of large-scale energy generation rather than become household items, but remote communities may find that they are actually a good solution for their electrical needs.

Even if you don't install high technology solutions, it's good to remember that simply opening a window for summer ventilation or installing a roof light for daylight means that you are part of the renewable energy community and are helping to reduce dependency on fossil fuels.

SUSTAINABLE MATERIALS
The style, materials and colour of your personal possessions mark out your own tastes, while the cracks, chips and grime give you a clue as to how well your choices have stood the test of time.

Look around your home to see what furniture is working well and where the chips and cracks are appearing. You will soon discover how solid timber furniture can be dented and knocked and still retain a certain pride, while laminated surfaces chip easily at corners exposing rough and ugly MDF. Cast iron pots last well when you compare them to the slicker aluminium pans with non-stick finishes which always seem to fail eventually. Plastic electrical sockets gather grime and you'll wish you forked out that little extra for chrome or brass fittings. Look continuously, not at the surface of your possessions, but at their depth and flexibility.

LIVING THE THREE RS
The ecological mantra, reduce, reuse, recycle, describes a set of ideas which helps you to conserve resources in your home and to decrease the mounting piles of waste being dumped in landfill sites around the world every day. Nature works in a cycle so that waste becomes food for other living systems, and we should try to do the same in our homes.

Reduce
To limit your material consumption and therefore decrease the strain on the world's resources, choose products that are long-lasting and have minimal packaging. Buy in bulk and borrow or hire occasional items rather than buying them (the average household drill is said to be used for only half an hour in its lifetime). Hiring a car will save money and energy, while giving you the choice of vehicle depending on your need, for example, a van for collecting furniture or a small car for visiting family and friends. In fact, it won't be long before companies that used to sell fridges will be selling a year's worth of cooling, recycling components when your fridge needs to be repaired and installing more efficient parts when they become available.

Reuse
Get into the reusing swing by purchasing high quality second-hand furniture. Repair appliances and furniture rather than throwing

them away. Keep a strong plastic bag and use this for grocery shopping instead of the countless, flimsy bags supplied by most supermarkets. Use washable plates and cutlery for picnics and outings instead of plastic disposable ones. Cut up old plastic bottles and use them in the garden to protect growing plants. Replace the covers on a worn sofa and, if you've had enough of it, give it to a charity or

hope house

The English architect, Bill Dunster, has designed an attractive and ecofriendly home and work space. Its key features include the south-facing, triple storey glazed atrium that stores heat, the mono-pitched metallic roof and the weather board upper storeys, providing light, air and lots of warmth.

< long-lasting

Sustainable materials, such as wood and clay, are safe, plentiful and long-lasting. Used creatively, they not only make beautiful and practical furniture and fittings, but also age well.

a house clearance shop where it will find a second home.

Recycle

Finally, choose items that can easily be recycled or upgraded when they come to the end of their lives. Buy solid monolithic furniture that can be dismantled and recycled once you have finished with it. This reduces landfill waste and the need to dig up more metals from the earth, cut down more forests or synthesise more oil to make plastics.

One way to encourage recycling is by buying products with recycled components. These vary from recycled office paper to terrazzo floor tiles made from old wine bottles.

LIVING WITH THE SEASONS

Nowadays, we often wear tee-shirts in midwinter and work in artificially lit and air-conditioned offices and shops in summer. When our lives are dominated by artificial environments it's easy to lose touch with the changing seasons and even the line between day and night can become blurred.

Rather than accepting this, design your home so that you live your life in tune with the seasons.

Eat fresh salads and berries in summer and vegetable stews in winter. If you have the space, build an unheated lean-to greenhouse and use it for growing plants in spring and as an extra room in warmer weather. Go out in the garden or a park during warm seasons and come the winter, snuggle up together with family and friends. All these things will not only create a more active and varied home experience, but will save energy and resources.

CREATING GREEN SPACE

Our cities are covered in asphalt and concrete and our lives are overwhelmed by electronics and artificial media. Often the only plants we see are imported cut flowers and bedraggled street trees fighting off the smog of urban pollution. Finding time and space to create green space is one way to combat this urban shock and give something back to nature. A garden, balcony or any outdoor space is worth its weight in gold in our crowded cities and we should use them to encourage flora and fauna. Equally, keeping plants inside our home will help to clean the air and provide colour, perfume and herbs.

Gardening shouldn't be seen as a battle against nature and disorder but as a search for balance between the weather, the soil, flora and fauna. If you make a careful, initial selection of the plants, they will require no more than pruning and occasional weeding. The resulting wild-flowers, trees and hedges will provide a varied environment of sun, shade and shelter at different scales. Plants that will grow successfully depend on the garden climate, the quality of the underlying soil and how much space and time you have for caring for them.

WHAT NEXT?

Many people and organisations are providing inspiring ways to improve our relationships with each other and the natural world, and I hope this book does the same. Chapter 2, Essential elements, examines the location and structure of your home, and explores how you can use light, colour and texture efficiently and creatively. In addition, it explains how to maintain healthy air and water and gives advice on

> garden gorgeous
This potential ecological resource improves the local climate, enriches the soil, encourages birds and insects to live and can also provide you with seasonal fruits and vegetables.

choosing energy-efficient and safe systems for heating, cooling and powering your home.

Chapter 3, Eco-materials, considers the environmental credentials of the materials used to build and furnish homes, explaining why materials matter, both locally (for your own health and comfort) and globally (for the planet and distant communities).

Chapter 4, Rooms for living, looks at all the areas of your home and how you can improve these, no matter what your style or budget, while Chapter 5, People

and pets, looks at changing your home to accommodate the changing lives of its inhabitants.

Chapter 6, Upkeep, looks at how we can maintain and clean our homes without it costing the earth, while Chapter 7, The Eco-rating Guide, provides an overall eco-score for many of the materials and products found in the book.

I hope *The Ecofriendly Home* provides a clearer understanding of how you can make positive choices in and around your home to encourage a sustainable future. Just as importantly, I hope you enjoy the read and your homes.

< warm and cosy
Instead of turning up the heating on cold days, wear a jumper, drink a hot soup or go for a run!

Essential elements

'There is a circle of questions with a very large circumference and no centre. And what all these questions come to is, "how am I to live?"' *The Man Without Qualities*, volume 3, Robert Musil.

The possibilities for choosing where to live and how to renovate your home are endless. Whether you live in a hot or cold climate, are old or young, buying somewhere new or old, renovating your home from top to bottom or are simply needing to rejuvenate one or two rooms, this chapter advises you on the essential elements of your home, helping you to fill in your own circle.

Chapter Two

Surveying
your home

If you are considering moving to a new home, you are in the fortunate position of being able to find somewhere with good eco-credentials. Estate agents might insist there are just three factors to choosing a home – location, location and location – but, while property moguls espouse post codes, we should really champion fresh air, clean water and natural light, as well as protection from the elements and a connection with the rhythms of the natural world. These ideals must also fit into your real life, being part of a valuable community, close to friends and family, and near to work and play.

The key to finding this ideal eco-home is to look for a well-designed building that sits comfortably in its surroundings, away from noise and pollution. It should make the most of the sun in winter and be sheltered from strong winds (and vice versa in hot climates). There should be good views from the windows, but also some privacy from neighbours. Make sure the ground on which it is built drains well, the building structure itself is sound, it is well insulated against noise and the weather, and there is enough space for all your needs.

Not all these criteria are visible to the untrained eye, so you may need a good surveyor (preferably one sympathetic to eco-principles) who can draw up a detailed report on the building before you commit yourself to buying.

While you can do little about your location if you're already settled in your home, there are still plenty of modifications you can make, both to your home and how you use it. These vary in scale from the major, such as building a conservatory or installing solar panels, to the minor, such as buying low-energy bulbs and fitting draught exclusion tape to door and window frames. Each adds, often invisibly, to the comfort and quality of your home.

< eco-elements
Sometimes it is obvious from the outside that a house has ecofriendly elements. At other times, you will need to examine its structure and surroundings more carefully to confirm this.

FACTORS TO CONSIDER

The table below provides a checklist of factors that can affect your home. Consider these when assessing the eco-worthiness of your home – be it old or new.

	Positive factors	Negative factors
Location	Quiet, unpolluted street	Noise and pollution from nearby roads or neighbour
	Close to green space	Urban jungle
	Multi-cultural	Mono-cultural
	Close to work, shops and leisure	Under electrical pylons or near sub-stations
	Personal outside space	No external space
	Tree-lined streets	Area affected by radon
	Good views	Overshadowing from surrounding buildings
	No light pollution at night	Badly designed street lights outside the house
Structure	Sound	Problematic
	Air-tight	Leaky doors, windows and walls
	Damp-proof	Musty air (a sign of damp penetration)
	Well insulated roof and walls (cavity construction with insulation)	Solid wall construction with no insulation
	Double glazing	Single glazing
	Good ventilation (windows opening onto clean streets)	Poor ventilation (few openable windows and those that do face stagnant spaces)
	All rooms with good natural light and high ceilings	Poor sunlight penetration (surrounded by tall buildings)
	South (sun-facing) or west aspect (in cool climates) or shaded aspect (in warm climates)	
	Just big enough	Too large or too small
Services	Efficient gas heating (in town) or wood fired high-efficiency stove (in country)	Electric heating
	Clean water pipes and tanks	Lead piping or broken drains

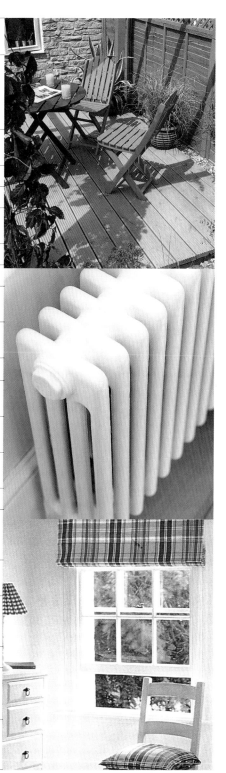

Making space

While materials, colour, light and texture define the surfaces of our homes, it is the space between the walls that holds the key to living well. To get a real feel for this space you need to live in it for a while. So, if you have moved to a new home, don't rush into instant renovations. Instead, do nothing for a while and simply watch how the space in each room changes through the day and the seasons. Scribble down notes and ideas, then discuss them with your partner, friends or other members of your household.

While you are doing this, set about correcting or improving the basics. This may include fixing structural defects, rewiring, re-plumbing, and sealing and insulating the building.

If the existing decorations are too much for your tastes, make some simple adjustments. Strip up old and dirty carpets (you may even be able to recycle them by giving them to a charity rather than throwing them away), or whitewash the walls and ceilings.

ALLOCATING ROOMS

Rooms are best laid out to harmonise with nature and any unchangeable man-made conditions. If you have the luxury of influencing the design of your

> take it slowly
If it is possible, keep some of your furniture in storage while you grow into your new home. Only then will the space between the walls trickle out and give you clues as to how you can proceed.

new home, or can assign rooms to specific directions, the first thing to consider is the time that you use each room and where the sun is in the sky through the day and through the seasons (see chart opposite). Other factors, such as the amount of noise and pollution each room receives from the street, whether there is a lot of overshadowing from trees or neighbouring buildings, and what the view is like also need consideration if the layout of your home is to work well.

A sunny disposition

Rooms warmed by the sun are more comfortable and require less heating, so use them as living or working spaces. Rooms that aren't should be reserved for bathrooms and storage space. In warmer climates practise the opposite.

Upstairs or downstairs?

While there may be practical reasons to keep common rooms at ground level and to place private

rooms above, this will not necessarily create the most inspiring plan. Since we spend more waking hours in our living rooms, the quality of natural light and the views these rooms have are more critical. Often the best place to gain these benefits is on the upper floors.

Equally, bedrooms are generally more contemplative spaces that need less light, so can therefore be sited on the lower floors. What's more, living rooms need to be warmer than bedrooms and, because warm air rises, the upper rooms are often warmer than ground floor spaces. Smells will also rise, so situating the kitchen on the top floor is a good idea as it is less likely to fill your home with the aroma of your last meal.

IDEAL ROOM LOCATIONS

The sun and wind have always been dominating influences on the home – cave dwellings were chosen to catch the sun in cold climates, while homes in the tropics were built with wide verandahs to shade them from sun and raised on stilts to catch breezes. Sunshine is a real mood booster, so make the most of it when planning your home. Below is a list of ideal room locations if you live in the northern hemisphere.

Room	Location
Bedrooms	Facing north east to south east to see the sun rising.
Kitchens and workrooms	South east to south west so they stay bright and airy in the day. If southern space is cramped, they can also be located to the north as these rooms often produce their own heat.
Living and dining rooms	South to north west so they are washed by the evening sun.
Gardens	Facing south-east to west so they are sunny in the afternoon and early evening.
Halls and utility rooms	North facing to act as a buffer against the cold in winter.
Bathrooms	East for morning people and west for evening people.

External noise

Noise and pollution from the street can spoil the overall harmony of your home, so less social rooms, such as the bathroom, should face the street. Make sure any windows in rooms that face a main road or busy street can be kept closed. Planting hedges, trees or building small utility spaces between your home and the road will help. If none of this is possible, then you'll have to deal with the noise by installing secondary window

> sound barriers

Tall plants and bushes will keep your garden private, shielding it from the gaze of curious onlookers. A living willow like this will also help to block out any noise and absorb pollution from nearby roads.

glazing. This will help to insulate your home in winter but lack of ventilation can also make it overheat in summer.

Overshadowing from adjacent buildings often cuts out sunlight, even from south-facing rooms. If this is the case with your home, paint the rooms a light colour to make the most of the reduced natural light and create warmth internally through the use of rich colours in furniture and fittings. You may even be able to create a skylight in the roof to brighten upper rooms.

CREATING MORE SPACE

Many homes were built for a completely different age, with rooms designed to suit different needs and different people. For example, many homes built in the 19th century were designed for large families who stayed together over a number of generations. This often led to houses with many small rooms, each functioning in ways particular to the cultural mores of that time. The kitchen was often small and separated from the dining room. There was frequently a playroom for the children and another for the adults, a room for special occasions and one for day-to-day use. Basements and upper floors were given far less height and partitioned off to become servants' quarters or bedrooms for the household's youngest children.

Many of these houses have now been converted into flats by developers who have installed even more partitions to create more rooms. One way to free up the potential of homes like these is by knocking down walls. Corridors and lobbies can become usable space, and light from the sunny side of your home can penetrate through to the areas of your home that are dark or overshadowed. Rooms that only supported one function can suddenly become multi-functional and fun.

Seeing this potential may take a little time and also require some serious investigation and expense on your part, but can often be a valuable addition to your home. Before you take down a wall, however, make sure you consult a surveyor or engineer (see page 65, Chapter 3).

Extensions

If you are lacking space, consider an extension to your home as this is often much cheaper than moving to a larger home. If you have a garage, park the car on the street and convert this room into a workshop. Alternatively, add some windows and good insulation to make it a study or spare bedroom. As well as adding value, major changes like these are an excellent opportunity to improve the overall efficiency of your home.

< creating a sunroom

If your home has a verandah, enclose it with windows to create a sunroom. The glass will capture the sun's heat and create a naturally warm space. This room is also good for growing plants all year round, bringing you closer to nature.

> opening up the roof

Create more space by installing skylights and insulation in the attic. With an external balcony, this room can have the best views in the whole house.

Expanding into the garden

The father of British self-build housing design, Walter Segal, built his first timber-framed house at the end of his garden. Many councils and local authorities allow you to build a small detached building within your garden without the need for planning consent, and it is often far easier and cheaper to build a small, self-contained garden building than it is to adapt your existing property. This ecofriendly retreat at the bottom of a north London garden was designed by the architect Sarah Wigglesworth.

Letting the light in

Light defines space, so it is important to understand how we can bring more natural light into our homes and use artificial light more creatively and economically. It is also important to understand how colour can complement light sources and subsequently the qualities of each room in your house.

The sun is the most efficient light source we have, yet we are no longer creatures of the day, so artificial light is just as important as natural light. Balancing the transparency and clarity of natural light with the subtle qualities of well-designed artificial lighting will create a home that works day and night, all year round.

SUNLIGHT

Economically, ecologically, emotionally and aesthetically, it is far better to use natural light throughout your home. Apart from the obvious fact that it is free and wastes no electricity, exposure to the sun has a positive effect on your emotional wellbeing. Lots of windows are the best way to spread daylight through your home. However, it's important to bear in mind that although huge windows may create bright homes, they also let the heat in and out, which means you need a huge boiler to keep warm in the winter and an air-conditioning system to keep cool in the summer.

> **rays of sunshine**
On a sunny day, aim to let as much natural light into your home as possible. White walls and polished floors reflect light, brightening the room even further.

Skylights are one good way to let sunlight into your home. These small roof-mounted windows can fill your entire hallway with light if placed at the top of staircases. Light pipes are also worth considering. These stainless steel pipes draw daylight deep into the centre of your home from glazed dome inlets on the roof and are particularly good for brightening up internal rooms. Simpler ways to bring more natural light into your home include using aluminium venetian blinds on windows, which can bounce light deep into a room. Fixing curtain rails that extend beyond the edge of the window and allow you to draw back the curtains fully will also make a difference to the amount of sunshine a room receives. Even decorating with light colours will brighten your home and reduce the need for artificial lights during the daytime.

ELECTRIC LIGHTING

The ability to transform space with the flick of a switch is one of the wonders of modern times, yet many lighting designers take this for granted and care little for the energy needed to reproduce the sun's stunning light effects. In an ecofriendly home, you have to try a little harder so that light follows function and form, and you are using efficient sources of light.

Suiting the mood

Rooms should be lit according to the task at hand, so make sure workrooms, kitchens and studies have more light than rooms used for relaxing, such as bedrooms and bathrooms. Also, rooms do not need to be washed in a constant light, so use lights in particular areas for specific purposes: a bedside light for reading, a desk lamp for studying or a work top light for food preparation. These pools of light not only allow you to work while your family relax, but also create an ambience that is far more pleasant than the general glow from a single ceiling fitting.

TECHNOLOGY

fluorescent bulbs

These use less than a fifth of the energy needed by a standard tungsten bulb and last up to ten times longer. Electricity passes through the electrodes at each end of the sealed fluorescent tube, which contains mercury vapour in an argon gas. This generates electrons, which form an arc that knocks electrons in the mercury atoms out of their normal position. When the electrons return to their normal position, they produce ultraviolet (UV) light. These UV rays strike phosphor particles coating the wall of the tube, creating a fluorescent glow.

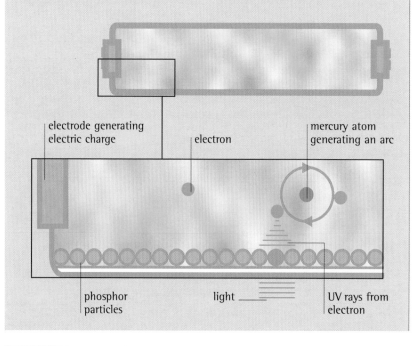

electrode generating electric charge

electron

mercury atom generating an arc

phosphor particles

light

UV rays from electron

Also, as the Japanese writer Tanizaki advocated in his book, *In Praise of Shadows*, the mystery and depth of shadow is just as important as light in creating a suitable atmosphere. So, where possible, choose lamps which allow you to alter the direction of light to suit your needs. A well designed desk lamp can be pointed over your head for reading or twisted round to wash the wall and create a background glow.

Diffuse light is more relaxing on the eye than a single bulb, so use a translucent lamp shade or throw light up onto the ceiling or onto a wall. Uplights need more power than a downlight and should only be used as low power background lighting in combination with other local sources of light.

Energy efficient lights

Ninety per cent of all household electric lights use standard tungsten bulbs. These consume a quarter of all the electricity needed in the home, yet they produce nine times more heat than light making them little more than inefficient electric heaters that also happen to glow a little. What's more, they only last a thousand hours before burning out. Luckily, there are plenty of alternatives which are just as attractive, last far longer and use less energy.

Ceiling lights are the most efficient form of light because they throw light directly at you, but

∧ lighting in situ
This large living space has several types of lighting for optimum adaptability. Skylights (with external blinds) allow natural light into the room, while downlighters create ambience. Spotlights display pictures to their best advantage and table lamps provide pools of light by each sofa. To save energy, always turn lights off when not needed.

LIGHTING EFFICIENCY SCALE

Below is a comparative list of the efficiency, duration and running cost of various home lighting options. (It's all over for the standard light bulb!)

Light source	Comparative efficiency	Life (hours)	Running cost each year
Daylight	100%	Forever	Zero
Fluorescent	20%	10000	Low
Halogen	8%	5000	Medium
Standard tungsten	4%	1000	High

they only work well if they are directly over the area of activity at hand. A light that hangs low over the dining table is good, but one that sits in the middle of the room over nothing in particular won't be very useful or efficient.

The best lighting options are compact and linear fluorescent bulbs (see page 26). Unlike older versions, which flickered for a few seconds before coming on, modern compact fluorescent bulbs start almost instantaneously and have colour rendering similar to tungsten bulbs so that they generate a warmer light instead of

< lighting options

A table lamp (top) not only provides a soft, sympathetic light but also adds a decorative element to a room. A string of recycled television screens (middle) creates a modern installation, while coloured wall washers (below) bathe textured walls in a gentle ambient glow.

the traditional blue, cool light which was thought to cause headaches. Most can't be dimmed easily but you can now buy linear tubes with dimmers.

If you want to light a single object, such as your favourite painting, 12-volt halogen bulbs are good alternatives. These have a very white, punchy light and are twice as efficient as tungsten bulbs. They can be bought with integral transformers as well as wire tracks, which allow you to fit them without having to also take down the ceiling.

By swapping to fluorescent or halogen lights, you will not only create a more attractive and varied home, but will also reduce your electricity bill by about a fifth, prevent the manufacture of around 150 normal bulbs and reduce carbon dioxide output from power stations by around 1500 kg a year.

Encouraging clean air

Invisible and all around us, air fills our home, carrying sound, smell, pollution and fire. If you relish the positive aspects of air and banish the negative, not only will your home smell cleaner, but you will also feel healthier too.

A good source of fresh air is vital for our wellbeing and the air inside our homes will only ever be as good as the air outside and is often far worse. When you walk in from the front street, your shoes bring with them dirt and grime. In fact, according to the World Resource Institute, 95 per cent of the lead and pesticide found in our homes comes in on our shoes.

AVOIDING AIR POLLUTION

One way of filtering outside air is to grow a leafy hedge between the street and your home. This will absorb some of the pollution and act as a noise barrier. The best approach, however, is to start a no-shoes policy at home. Put a shoe rack by your front door and provide socks and slippers for family guests. This may take time to become a habit, but it will cut down on your cleaning time and definitely be worth it in the end.

Since pollution is worse by roads, always try to open windows that are facing away from the main road. Air from the back of the home might not necessarily be clean, but it will nearly always be better than air straight from the street. Many local councils have realised that street pollution is one of the chief causes of ill-health and are implementing measures to reduce traffic and the resulting pollution in residential areas.

Gas, coal and wood-burning fires and cookers are all potential

< up the garden path
If you live in a built-up residential area, use a coir door mat or have a front path made from wood chippings, sand or sea shells to clean the grime from your shoes before entering your home.

sources of air pollution, especially if they produce smoke or if you allow the gases to come into your home. If they are sealed, have controlled air inlets and flues leading outdoors, and are properly maintained, they should not be a problem. Although smoky fuels are generally very bad for your health, smokeless fuels can be even more harmful because you can't see the pollution they produce. Poorly maintained gas fires with bad ventilation and air-starved heaters create carbon monoxide which can kill silently while you're asleep. If your kitchen has a gas cooker, make sure you have a good

extract ventilation system to prevent the build up of dangerous combustion gases, such as carbon monoxide and nitrogen dioxide, and buy a carbon monoxide detector to be safe.

Radon

In some parts of the world, pollution also seeps in from the ground in the form of radon, a naturally occurring radio-active gas. Radon rises from underground rocks and flows into homes through poorly sealed floors. Local authorities will be able to tell you whether radon is a problem in your area and will also advise on

how to reduce its risk. The basic method for reducing radon is to seal the ground floor and draw underground gases away from your home by either extracting air from an underground well or from the void under a raised timber ground floor. Good ventilation in the home will also help to reduce radon and you can even consider installing a heat recovery ventilation system that provides a constant but low-energy air cleaning system (see page 40).

Natural air fresheners

Rather than use mass-produced air fresheners, keep your home clean and fresh by choosing non-toxic furniture and floor finishes, avoiding damp build-up in bathrooms and kitchens, and by implementing a non-smoking policy. If you want to scent the air, use fresh flowers, herbs and essential oils. Suitable flowers that add a pleasant aroma to your surroundings include fresh-cut honeysuckle, jasmine and rose flowers. Crush fresh lavender, thyme and lemon balm and keep them in a bowl in different parts of the home to benefit from their scent. Burning essential oils such

< kitchen freshness
An extractor hood above the hob will absorb cooking smells and remove excess heat, preventing these from spreading to other parts of your home.

as sandalwood and amber or adding them to soaps will also help to cover up any unpleasant cooking odours in your home.

Ionisers

Thought by some people to keep the air cleaner, ionisers come in two types. The simpler one draws in air and gives particles of dust a negative charge. Walls and floors in the room become relatively positively charged and dirt is then attracted to the nearest surface. This results in cleaner air but dirtier walls. However, you will at least be able to see the dirt to clean it away. The negatively charged air also counteracts the positive charges that come off electrical equipment.

The second type is an electrostatic filter that ionises the air but also contains a positively charged filter element which catches dust as it passes through the machine. The air that returns to the room should consequently be neutral and clean.

There is little scientific evidence that ionisers will really improve your life, but many people swear by them. If you've tried everything else and failed, then borrow an ioniser from a friend or ask to test-drive one before purchasing.

VENTILATION

Many specialists feel that modern homes are under-ventilated and consequently prone to internal

pollution. In fact, very few homes are completely air-tight and many leak like a sieve. This is true for old and new buildings alike, and some older buildings often feel like they are more air than wall! The only air-tight buildings have been specially built by green architects who use high-quality techniques to seal every gap in the outside wall. As these are rare, you should assume that if your home is stuffy or makes you ill, the problem is more likely to do with the materials and appliances in your home (see Chapter 3) or how your home is mechanically ventilated.

Rooms that do require additional ventilation are bathrooms, toilets and kitchens. In essence, you should have a positive extract ventilation system to remove smells, control dampness and pollution, and to ensure that heat is not wasted by opening windows in cold weather. Heat recovery systems can also be used to improve the quality of ventilation in your home.

< household helpers
One of the best-known indoor air cleaners is the spider plant, whose leaves absorb formaldehyde from carpets. Chrysanthemums and azaleas are also known to remove chemicals from the air during photosynthesis, while perfuming your home in the process.

Other ventilation options are trickle vents that are found in many modern homes. These let air into a room without the need to open any windows. They can be fitted with small sliders so you can adjust the level of ventilation to suit the changing climate and your personal requirements.

Dampness

Poor ventilation is just one of the causes of damp air and surfaces, a problem that can make our homes smell, encourage microbes and cause asthma and bronchial illnesses. To solve damp problems, find the cause rather than treat the effect. As well as poor ventilation, damp in modern buildings is caused by hidden leaks and poor building work. In older buildings, damp can also occur if water penetrates solid walls or rises through unsealed ground floors. If you can't find the cause of your problem, seek the advice of an independent surveyor. Damp from faulty plumbing or leaking drains, flashing and tiles can be resolved by fixing the problem at source. As for damaged or missing damp-proof membranes (plastic or rubber sheets that stop buildings from getting wet), these should be replaced and all surfaces will need to be treated with damp-repellent paints. Unfortunately, some damp-proofing techniques may create pollution themselves. The worst culprits are chemical injection kits that stop damp from rising in external brickwork. Far better than these, although more expensive, is inserting a new damp proof course in the faulty area using traditional materials such as slate.

∨ an airy room

Well-designed windows provide controlled access to daylight and clean, fresh air. Open them in summer for a cool breeze, but use trickle vents in the winter to prevent heat loss. Ventilation is vitally important if you have a hobby involving potentially toxic materials, such as glues or paints. Better still choose ecofriendly paints.

Conserving
water

Water, like air, is vital to our lives. Yet so often it is demoted to a dull necessity, left to be dealt with by plumbers and forgotten when decorating. Water is, in fact, one of the most calming and cleansing elements available, both creatively and ecologically.

Rather than relying totally on the complex set of reservoirs, chemical treatment, pumping stations, pipework, sewers and sewage outfall created by national utility companies, we can put some of our faith in the natural cycle of water. This involves collecting rainwater from our roofs, storing it safely in cool underground tanks and using it for much of our water needs. Combined with sensible conservation techniques, our demand for water can be reduced by at least 50 per cent. At the same time we can create an exciting addition to our homes.

HARVESTING RAIN WATER

The roof of a typical European home can collect enough water to supply a family of three with most of its annual water needs.

The first stage of reusing rainwater is to simply store it in a couple of plastic butts for use in the garden or for washing outdoor equipment. The next stage is to

collecting water
Water can be collected and recycled on a small scale (above), or a larger-scale tank (right) collects water for most of a household's needs.

construct a plastic or concrete tank underground where the water will remain cool and clean. The temperature is an important aspect because dangerous bacteria does not grow in cool water.

While rainwater is basically safe, many areas of the world (cities especially) have high levels of air pollution, making the direct use of rainwater for drinking potentially harmful (although it can be filtered). Rainwater quality is much better in rural areas, but you still need to ensure that the roof collecting it is lead-free. Check that all lead flashings have been removed and that the roof is not made from zinc or asbestos.

DRINKING WATER

We only drink 3 per cent of the water delivered to our homes, yet it is all purified and chemically treated at vast expense, sometimes even to dubious quality. This water is often treated with chlorine and

ECOTIP

Water safety
Even in the developed world, water borne diseases remain a constant threat. To prevent this, inspect your water tank regularly, keeping an eye out for water stagnation. Also, make sure that all your pipework and fittings are clean and scale-free. If cold water is stored below 15°C and hot water above 55°C, then any bacteria either die or lie dormant. If water is between these temperatures, you are at risk of legionnaire's disease (a form of pneumonia), especially if you are old or unwell.

< washing up by hand
If you generate only a small amount of dirty dishes, it is more ecological and economical to wash dishes by hand.

fluorine, which is good for teeth, but some people find the taste unpleasant. Buying bottles of imported mineral water is not an ecological solution as the energy used to manufacture and transport it is far less efficient than treating tap or rainwater. Simple jar-based carbon filters are a cheap and relatively effective way to improve the taste of drinking water, but make sure you change the filter frequently. You can also buy more expensive whole house or tap-based filter systems that provide a one-stop solution for removing hardness from water, while also ensuring it is chemically clean.

HOUSEHOLD APPLIANCES

One of the great successes of environmental awareness has been the development of household appliances that combine time-saving effectiveness with ecological respect. While some manufacturers have always considered water and energy consumption an important part of

the design, the majority felt that price and look were the only selling points. Now that Europe, Scandinavia and America have developed eco-labelling and Energy Star certification, we can see clearly how one product compares with the others. If we all choose A-rated appliances and use them wisely, we will not only save money in the short term, but we will also help to reduce the effects of pollution and water shortage on our planet in the future.

Dishwashers
While older dishwashing machines used large quantities of water, A-rated dishwashers actually save more water and energy than washing up by hand. This is because they sense the dirtiness of the water and decide whether it can be used twice. They also use hot water from one cycle to warm the water in the next, and use cold water to condense steam so the dishes can be dried with air alone. These new dishwashers can clean a whole day's dirty dishes with less than fifteen litres of water (see page 166, Chapter 6). Dishwashers require far harsher detergents than washing up liquid, but ecofriendly alternatives are available.

Washing machines

Albeit great labour-saving devices, washing machines have only recently become water and energy efficient. Like dishwashers, A-rated washing machines monitor the dirtiness of rinse water, recycle hot water, and have numerous settings to cater for different loads. They still consume over 50 litres of water for each wash, so it is best to save your dirty laundry until you have a full load and dry your clothes on the line rather than tumbling them in a restricted drier; they'll smell fresher, have fewer creases and save energy.

WATER PIPES

In the past, before its toxicity was common knowledge, water pipes were made of lead. If your house is more than 40 years old, check that the pipe-work has been replaced because water running through lead can cause this metal to accumulate in the body, resulting in mental retardation, hypertension and impaired immune response. The most ecofriendly piping available today is polypropylene plastic for hot water pipes and polyethylene for cold water systems. These materials do not corrode and their production uses less energy than steel or copper pipes. Stainless steel pipes may be preferable for exposed locations as they are attractive and are easy to recycle at the end of their lives. Copper

LIVING NATURALLY

Conserving water

The average household uses about 160 litres of water per day, all of which is treated, pumped, then dumped. The following are some simple practices that can reduce this figure:
• Never let tap water run when drinking it. Use a glass instead.
• Use a plug in kitchen sinks and bathroom basins.
• Fix leaking taps immediately and consider installing aerating taps that halve water flow.
• Run a bath only when you have the time to luxuriate in it and share it with someone!
• Don't use kitchen waste disposal units because these waste water and also throw away valuable compost.
• Have quick showers instead of a bath and avoid power showers.
• Install a dual flush loo, which gives you the option of flushing with a small or a large dose of water. Alternatively, put a brick in the cistern. A more radical option is to install a zero water toilet.
• Collect and filter rainwater (see page 33) to use in baths, showers, washing machines and gardens.

pipes are still commonly used as they are well understood by the trade, but they do cause some water pollution which is harmful to water-borne organisms.

All hot water pipes should be insulated to keep water warm, and the distance between the hot water store and taps should be as short as possible. If you live in a cold climate, you should also insulate cold water pipes and tanks in lofts and basements to prevent them from freezing and bursting.

Ceramic remains the best material for drains as it creates less pollution during production than plastic alternatives. If you use plastic drains, avoid pvc as this is more toxic and harder to dispose of than polypropylene.

RESTORATIVE QUALITIES

In Eastern philosophies, water is a very important element. It is also a key factor in design, both in the home and in the garden. In winter, leave wide bowls of water with incense or floating candles to create a relaxing atmosphere in a room and add moisture to dry air. In summer, follow an old Indian custom and fill leaky clay pots with water, then wrap them in muslin cloth and leave by an open window sill. The breeze will evaporate the water, thus chilling the air.

In the garden, water supports a diverse range of flora and fauna, from reeds and lilies to frogs and water boatmen. These come into their own during summer, when the garden pool becomes a thriving living community.

If you have a large garden, clean and reuse waste water from sinks and baths by installing a reed bed filtering system. If you are going to do this, don't use dangerous chemicals in your house, such as chlorine and ammonia (see page 165, Chapter 6 for alternatives). Drain grey water (the term for water from sinks and baths) from

∧ soothing water

The sound of trickling water makes your garden a calming and supportive place in which to spend time. Rather than feeding an outdoor water feature or pond with chlorinated tap water, maintain it with rainwater from your roof or divert water from hard paving in the garden.

your home into a gravel bed where reeds and other water-loving plants are grown. Bacteria that feed on nutrients in the water will help to break down the more complex chemicals, and water from the reed bed will eventually drain through the gravel to a second bed, then into a pond that can feed other garden plants or else flow safely away into soakaways or streams.

Heating
your home

In the temperate world, half of all the energy consumed in the home is used for heating, yet with careful design it is quite possible to halve this figure. In cities, the best heating systems to have are gas-fired ones, while wood boilers are good for country homes. Never use electricity for heating because it creates three times as much pollution as a high-efficiency gas boiler. Other inefficient heating sources include older gas fires and boilers and coal-effect gas fires. Open coal or wood-burning fires are also inefficient, not to mention polluting, so avoid these as well. The best eco-option is to have solar panels, but your home needs to have a south-facing garden or roof. These will preheat water, but they are quite expensive, so make sure you consider the simpler and cheaper options first.

INSULATION

Just like a warm coat, a cosy home needs to be well insulated with tight-fitting openings. The cost of insulating your home depends on the way it was originally built. Simple techniques, such as roof insulation, will pay back in one or two years, while major renovations, such as double glazing, take ten years to recoup the original outlay. The benefits in terms of comfort, energy saving and ecological responsibility are well worth considering, however.

Roofs

These are the easiest part of the home to insulate, particularly if you have an attic. Cellulose insulation is made from recycled paper and 150 to 200 millimetres of it will reduce to almost zero the heat lost through your roof. The paper is pre-treated with environmentally sensitive fire and animal repellent and is blown into the roof void via an air-blower

> a warm glow
Fireplaces provide a focal point in many homes, but should be used sparingly as they are inefficient and create pollution. In mild weather though, lighting a fire in the sitting room may be more efficient than turning on the central heating.

(basically a vacuum cleaner in reverse). The paper lies in the space, keeping heat in and reducing noise from rain.

Other eco-insulation materials include sheep's wool (marketed as Climawool) and corkboard. Less benign materials include glass and mineral fibre mats, various expanded plastics and loose-fill heat blown vermiculite.

When insulating roofs, remember to keep eave vents clear so that moisture doesn't build up and cause damage from condensation. You should also carry out all carpentry, plumbing and electrical works before laying down insulation. Finally, make sure you protect insulation from hot flues, recessed lighting and electrical wiring to avoid heat damage.

DEGREES OF ENERGY SAVING

When it comes to energy saving, it's best to start with simple measures which have a large impact, then move towards more complex and expensive tasks.

Simple changes

Fit draught-excluding strips around window and door frames.
Fit heavy curtains to windows and close them at night.
Place door stoppers by doors.
Fill gaps under skirting boards with newspaper or sealant.
Install additional insulation in the loft space.
Insulate the hot water tank and hot water pipes.
Install a time clock and thermostat for your heating system.

Medium-effort changes

Install thermostatic radiator valves on room radiators.
Build a draught lobby for front and back doors.
Add thermal stores to catch the heat in sun-facing rooms.

Changes requiring significant effort and money

Replace old boilers or electric heating systems with modern high-efficiency condensing gas or wood-fired boilers.
Replace old and leaky windows with new double glazed units or install secondary windows behind traditional hard-to-replace windows in older homes.
Add solar conservatories to sun-facing rooms and buffer spaces to north facing ones.

More expensive solutions

Fit solar panels on the roof and south facing walls.
Add additional insulation to walls and floors.
Install a home heat recovery system to replace individual extract fans in kitchens and bathrooms.

Floors

The simplest way of insulating ground floors is to install insulation under the final floor covering. From an ecological perspective, the greenest material is corkboard because it is a naturally renewable material. It is also water and vermin resistant and easy to lay. The cheapest material for floor insulation is probably expanded polystyrene board. This provides good insulation and is also easy to lay, but its environmental credentials are not as good as cork.

If you have a raised timber ground floor then you can achieve very good insulation by installing cellulose fibre between the floor joists. This is simply lain on top of a breather layer or fibreboard which is supported from the joists. Make sure that you do not block air vents as this will cause damp and consequent damage.

Windows

Area for area, windows are the most leaky part of your home. A single sheet of glass provides hardly any insulation at all. Double glazing, by contrast, traps a layer of insulating air between the two panes of glass, halving the amount of heat loss compared with single-glazed windows. Even more energy-conserving types of window are now available. One of these is known as low e (emissivity) glazing. This consists

∧ **keeping the heat in**
Thick and lined floor-to-ceiling curtains keep heat in and draughts out, while adding colour and texture to your home. If you have radiators beneath your windows, it is a good idea to move them to an internal wall, otherwise much of the heat they produce will escape outside.

Most modern external walls are made from cavity walls that comprise two brick or concrete blocks with a void in between. These can be insulated (if they aren't already) by injecting mineral fibre into the void. While not an environmentally benign process, the resulting reduction in your heat and energy expenditure make it a good long-term option.

Older homes built with solid walls can be insulated by installing an internal or external lining of insulation. Internal insulation involves building a wall of timber battens against the external walls that need insulation. Cellulose fibre or mineral fibre panels fill the cavity between the battens, and the wall is then covered in a final layer of

of a thin layer of transparent plastic film between the panes of glass which bounces heat back into the room. Another option is to choose glazed windows with argon gas (a better insulator than air) between the panes. The really eco-conscious may prefer triple-glazed windows with argon gas and low e film; these let more heat into your home than they lose, which, in effect, make them heaters without an annual bill!

If you are in the enviable position of building your own home, it will be more energy-efficient to install more windows on sun-facing elevations and fewer on northern facing ones (and obviously the reverse if you live in the southern hemisphere). Remember, however, to provide some shading on south or west facing windows as this will prevent your home from overheating in summer.

Walls

Insulating walls is more complex but can be just as important, particularly if your home is in a cold, windy and exposed location.

∧ **warm walls**
A fully renewable natural material, wool makes an excellent insulant. It is highly efficient at trapping air and therefore heat, absorbs moisture from the air and also provides sound insulation.

plasterboard. The down side of internal insulation is that rooms become slightly smaller, but a small warm room is far better than a large cold one!

External insulation is often applied to homes that are badly affected by damp. This involves fixing mineral fibre slabs to the outside walls, then rendering the surface with plaster to create a water and damage-resistant finish which you can paint.

EFFICIENT HEATING

If your home is small and well-insulated, it is best to concentrate all your heating in one room and let adjacent rooms warm up by heat's natural movement through walls and air. One way of achieving this is by installing a small gas or wood-fired stove in the living room, which is where you spend most of your time. Wood stoves (see below right) with secondary combustion chambers

TECHNOLOGY

heat recovery systems

These suck warm stale air out of rooms, absorbing the heat from the air into a metal heat exchanger and transferring the warmth into fresh air, which is then blown into living rooms or circulation spaces. Homes with these systems have lower heating bills and are free from draughts, provided that windows are properly sealed and trickle vents closed. The one downside is that the running fans can consume more energy than is saved by recovering heat. To avoid this, buy units with small variable speed fans sized for your needs and use humidity controlled grilles that turn the unit off when air is dry.

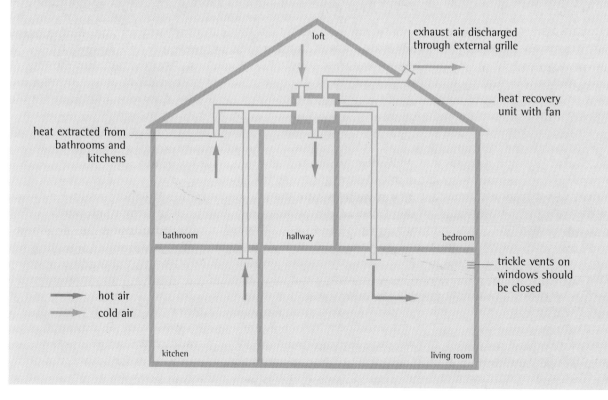

loft

exhaust air discharged through external grille

heat recovery unit with fan

heat extracted from bathrooms and kitchens

bathroom

hallway

bedroom

trickle vents on windows should be closed

hot air
cold air

kitchen

living room

will halve the amount of logs required and reduce emissions through the chimney.

In larger homes, it is probably best to install a central heating system with a single boiler and radiators in each room. A good central heating system uses a condensing boiler, so-called because even the heat in the exhaust gas is condensed out of them. Condensing boilers are 90 per cent efficient, saving you significant sums of money and energy over their lifetime. If you are installing the system from scratch, design it to run at a low temperature (40–50°C rather than the traditional 70–80°C) as this ensures the boiler is running at high efficiency all the time.

To control when the boiler operates, use a timer and easily adjustable thermostat. You can also install thermostatic radiator valves, which allow you to set the temperature in each room. Boiler manufacturers have developed complex controls; the more you spend, the more functions you have and these programmable controllers are definitely cost-effective in larger homes.

A low-energy alternative to radiators is under floor heating. Plastic heating pipes are fitted into the floor, either in a cement screed or in chip-board panels. Because they warm the floor rather than the air, homes with under floor heating can be kept a couple of degrees cooler, which will save you up to 20 per cent of your heating bill.

Efficient hot water

Generally, hot water uses the same boiler as your heating system. In older homes, boilers heat hot water tanks, which are fed from a separate cold water tank in the loft. These systems tend to lose lots of heat through the miles of copper tubing employed in their design. If your home has this system, keep the tank and pipes well insulated, set the tank thermostat at 55°C and use a time switch which only turns the boiler on when you need hot water.

< cosy warmth
Wood burning stoves not only heat the room they occupy, they can also generate enough energy to warm water.

In new homes, you may find that mains pressure combination condensing boilers provide a more efficient source of warm water. Commonly known as combi boilers, these only fire up when there is a demand for warm water, although good ones will have a mini storage tank so you don't have to wait for hot water to appear at the tap.

SOLAR HEATING

While winter is often cold and dark, there are still many days when the sun comes out. On these days, sun-facing rooms in your home can collect heat and solar stores can trap the heat for later in the day. Solar stores are dark, heavy surfaces inside the home that warm up when hit by the sun. At night they keep rooms warmer without the need for additional heating. Heavy-weight homes that have concrete floors and brick walls are natural solar stores. Light-weight homes of timber and plasterboard require a little more ingenuity. Some architects place barrels of water inside rooms as these have a huge thermal mass which absorbs heat well. If the floor can take the weight, another option is to lay slates or tile walls in sunny parts of your home.

∧ the old and the new

You don't need to live in an ultra-modern home to consider solar-powered heating. In fact, the only requirement is that you have a south-facing roof that gets plenty of sunshine. Sometimes the clean design of solar panels can actually complement more traditional architectural styles.

Solar-powered hot water

If your home has a south-facing roof or sunny garden, installing solar panels can halve your hot water bill and provide you with free hot water throughout the summer. Some heat can even be collected on cloudy days, but you'll still need a gas or solid fuel boiler for a top up on winter days.

Solar panels are usually installed onto your roof where they collect the sun's energy and transfer the heat to your home's hot water storage tank. They are best located above any overshadowing trees or buildings and should face between south-east and south-west. Obviously, the amount of sunshine varies depending where you live, so this will affect the type of solar panel you need. There is a huge range, each with its own pros and cons. Evacuated tube systems are more expensive but are also more efficient, while flat plate systems are cheaper but larger. You can even make your own by painting radiators black and putting them in a poly tunnel in the garden.

The amount of money you save will depend on the type of heating system you have. If you have a gas boiler, it will take around 20 to 30 years to pay back the money invested in solar panels, but knowing you are doing your bit for the environment will make the investment worthwhile.

Keeping
cool

In warm climates, the number of homes with air-conditioning is growing at an alarming rate. While this modern facility gives a perceived improvement in comfort over the short term, it creates a highly artificial environment and brings with it many health risks. It is much better instead to make use of natural passive cooling.

The ideal way to protect your home from over-heating is to use plants as shade providers, breeze collectors and climate modifiers. A

keep your cool
Wooden shutters (above) keep sunshine out while allowing breezes to circulate. A pergola (right) offers some welcome shade.

LIVING NATURALLY

Protection from the sun

If your home is over-heating because of a poorly designed roof, consider the following:

• Installing heat reflecting aluminium foil and insulation in the attic space or under the roof tiles to reduce heat build up in the roof.

• Increasing ventilation to the attic space by adding some louvres and wind chimneys which catch the prevailing breeze.

• Building your roof out over sun-facing east and west sides of your home to protect it from direct sunlight.

• Painting metal roofs a light colour to reflect more of the heat. Special paints that reflect more than two thirds of the sun's heat are now available in most hardware stores.

good planting scheme can reduce the temperature of the ground around your home by up to 10°C. Deciduous trees to the west and south will protect your home from the summer sun, but allow winter sun through. While plants won't prevent the heat from high-level midday sun, they will provide shade in the early morning and late afternoon. Tree and vine belts to the east and west of your home give the best protection. Vines and thick-leafed plants can also shade windows and walls from sun that is reflected off the ground.

SHADING YOUR HOME

By fixing external awnings to your windows, you not only keep solar heat out of the house, you also protect paint from peeling. Indoor blinds, slatted shutters or overhanging roofs use the same principle to keep you cool.

Pergolas are perhaps the simplest way of shading your home while

providing additional living space on dry days. These are best built from timber posts and beams that can support layers of shade cloth. They also provide surfaces for vines and climbers to grow along.

Once you have protected your home from the sun, you need to make the best use of the cool night air and prevailing winds to make your home comfortable on the hottest days. The windows and internal doors of your home should be designed so that breezes can flow through your house day

< cool cooking

An external awning and ceiling fan will help to keep the kitchen — usually the hottest room in the house — cool.

and night. You also need to consider associated issues, such as security, acoustics and protection from weather. If your windows have external slatted shutters, they should be burglar-proof with the windows opening inwards. Also, make sure external awnings and verandahs are designed to withstand strong winds and heavy rain. To make the most of night ventilation, your home should ideally be constructed of heavy surfaces which will absorb the cool of the night and so keep your home cooler in the day.

KEEPING COOL INDOORS

In hot and dry climates, reduce the temperature in your home by using evaporative water cooling. You can do this either by placing muslin-wrapped leaky clay jugs of water on window sills or by purchasing an evaporative cooler, which cools the air by spraying water into a fan-assisted air stream.

If all else fails, consider using air-conditioning for some of the time. Traditional through-the-wall units are inexpensive but inefficient solutions. Instead, buy air-conditioners with very high-efficiency compressors because these reduce electrical demand to a minimum. Also, only turn them on when absolutely necessary.

MADE IN GREECE

Cool interiors

In hot Mediterranean countries, houses are often designed with thick walls, small windows, internal courtyards and white rendered walls because these features provide comfortable living conditions without the need for expensive and energy consuming air-conditioning. Commonly found in Greece and Spain, these homes often have cooler interiors than modern air-conditioned hotels.

Colour, texture and pattern

A quick and easy way to stamp your unique personality on a space is by treating it to a few licks of paint and some interesting fabric throws.

CHOOSING COLOURS

To decide on a colour scheme, you need to understand how colour affects space and your moods. Because dark surfaces absorb light while light surfaces reflect it, dark colours make a room feel smaller, while light colours make a room seem larger. In the same way, dark colours absorb heat, so painting a sunny room in darker colours will make it warmer than painting it with a pale, light colour.

The ideal colour scheme for an eco-home would therefore vary depending upon the weather and the time of year. On dark days, light surfaces will help to brighten your home while on sunny winter days darker furnishings can be used in south facing rooms to capture some of the sun's warmth.

Natural colours

Nowadays you can get dyes in any colour under the sun, chiefly due to the amazing technical advances made in the chemical industry. The synthetic dye industry uses many heavy metal salts and oxides to make everything from brilliant

creative illusions

A large space will feel intimate and cosy if it is decorated with solid materials and dark colours (left). Similarly, a small space will have a light and airy atmosphere if it is decorated with pale colours (above).

white (titanium) to acid yellow (chrome). Yet, many of these metals are toxic and can pollute our water supply. Instead, we should be opting for natural dyes, which are not only beautiful, but also harmless.

Earth pigments are based on colours found in natural earth sources and vary in colour from traditional browns, such as burnt sienna and red ochre, to deep greys and blacks. Mineral

pigments are created using similar techniques to the mainstream chemical industry but rely on known-to-be-safe minerals. These dyes are supplied as powder pigments which are mixed into neutral paints to create a huge variety of colours and shades. For more information on choosing paints and dyes see page 66, Chapter 3.

< colour swatches
Before you go ahead and choose a colour scheme, use colour swatches in varying shades to get a more complete feel for each of their effects.

Creating mood with colour

Although colour is a very personal experience, there are some general rules to follow when deciding on colour schemes for different parts of your home.

Bedrooms are restful calming places that need to work both on dark winter mornings and in the middle of summer. You should therefore decorate these rooms with light shades as they will encourage you to wake up. Avoid colours that are too cool, such as a bright blue, or warm reds and oranges, as these are either too stimulating or too lethargic.

Living rooms can afford to be painted in brighter colours, although neutral colour schemes will work equally well. Avoid strong colours over large areas

unless you are absolutely sure that they will work, either because you have seen them in a friend's home or on your travels.

A single wall of strong colour set off against a neutral background often works more successfully than a room immersed entirely in strong colour. Similarly, a common colour theme throughout your home will be more successful than a series of contrasting colours.

Neutral colours will frame and compose furniture, decorations and flowers more successfully than strong colour schemes, but bright colour schemes do work well with neutral furniture and decorations.

PATTERNS AND TEXTURES

In the same way as colour, different patterns and textures can influence the atmosphere, perceived space and mood of your home. If your rooms don't feel

> simple solutions
Incorporating texture and patterns into your home doesn't have to be an expensive or arduous job. Simple and natural elements can be used to great effect and minimal cost.

quite large enough, you could consider using patterned wallpapers and fabrics to create the illusion of space. Horizontal stripes help to widen a space, while vertical stripes can give the illusion of rooms having more height. Use these techniques carefully as the resulting pattern can overwhelm everything else. Although pattern en masse can be overwhelming, a wall of repeated form can create a stimulating backdrop in a neutral room.

Natural patterns

Throughout the ages, these have been inspirations for all kinds of artworks. You can bring them into your home directly by exposing the grain of wood in furniture and other objects, or by displaying the subtle and changing colours of polished or raw stones and slates. Hand-made fabrics coloured with plant dyes capture both the imagination of the designer and the accidental flaws of natural materials. Print and computer processes allow modern designers to uncover new natural patterns, with the fractal world of atomic particles and organic growth patterns found in leaves, shells and items of nature.

Texture

As well as pattern, texture is about touch and shape, and is a great way to bring the natural world into your home. A textural home is, in essence, a visual and tactile massage, the rough scratch of fibre rugs or the calm and cool surface of a sea-worn beach pebble. Introducing the flotsam and jetsam of the natural world into your home can make the plainest of corners a fond memory and a visual delight.

The texture of an item will affect how easy it is on the eye. Use soft-textured, light-absorbing materials such as fabrics to balance the harsher effects of reflective surfaces. And remember that shiny textures such as gloss paint or ceramic tiles will stand out more than velvety or rough textures such as brick.

∨ paint effects

You can add depth and warmth to your colour scheme by using special techniques for applying paint. Different brushes and combs will allow you to achieve a whole variety of effects, such as the 'denim' look of this bedroom wall.

Eco-materials

Materials matter. They provide us with a framework around which we build our homes and are the surfaces that we see, feel and walk on. Just as importantly, they impact on the world around us, improving or scarring the land, providing prosperity or poverty, health or illness, and creating beauty or ugliness. Your choice of materials should therefore be based on more than just price, convenience and fashion. Instead, consider how you can make your home connect with the world around you, capturing the beauty of the natural world and stimulating your senses and your mind.

Chapter Three

What makes an eco-material?

Eco-materials must reflect your own way of living and your particular take on the world. Without this, they will quickly bore you and be changed for something new (this throw-away culture is not particularly ecofriendly). For some, the fundamental choice of how to decorate and fill the home may create a place of softness and ease, for others, one of sparseness which provides room to think clearly and change rapidly.

There are a number of factors that determine eco-materials. They grow naturally or are plentiful; need little energy to make, deliver and care for; are non-toxic and easy to clean; are long-lasting; provide both local and global communities with decent livelihoods; and are easy to reuse when they come to the end of their lives. Often, they may be secondhand, passed down by older generations from a time when beauty, durability and craftsmanship were the only recognised ways of making things.

Similarly, good designs are healthy and ergonomic, lasting well beyond the dictates of fashion, and ageing with you. They are also safe for children and the less able. They might be made from recycled materials, but should always be practical, fun and tasteful.

> **hand me down**
Always try to buy classic, good-quality furniture made from long-lasting materials such as wood, metal or leather. These will not only serve you well throughout their lifetime in your home, but will also be appreciated down the family line for generations to come.

The guide on pages 174–183 provides an eco-rating for many of the materials you are likely to find around your home, and this chapter guides you through the range of materials you can choose to decorate and furnish your home. From the surfaces you stand on and lean against to the furniture you lounge on, the utensils you cook with, the fabrics you drape and the clothes you wear, and even the garden path you stroll along, you will discover what sort of materials are best

< **suitable materials**
Generally speaking, materials can be divided into four categories: those that grow naturally, such as wood, grasses and animal skins (top), those that are rare resources, such as metal and oil (far left), those that are plentiful and safe, such as stone, gravel and sand (immediate left), and finally, those that are toxic, such as lead or solvents. All but the toxic have a place in our homes.

suited to which rooms in or areas of your home, for your own and family's health, for ease of maintenance and also, of course, for the benefit of the planet.

Your personal circumstances will also affect the choices you make about the materials you choose for your home. Ask yourself how long you intend to stay where you live or how your life will change while you are there. What influences do your partner, your children or your work life have on how you live at home? If you are often on the move, choose small and portable furnishings that you can take with you. And if you have children, favour hard-wearing and easy-to-clean items.

Finally, no matter what the advertisers or eco-activists say, natural does not always mean good and synthetic doesn't always mean bad. It may, in fact, be better to build a house from recycled steel than from poorly managed forest timber and reuse ecofriendly plastic bags instead of recycled paper ones.

MATERIALS AND THEIR COMPARATIVE ENERGY USE

The energy needed to make finishes and furniture is one way to discover the environmental impact of goods we buy. The chart below shows the energy measured in Gigajoules (GJ) needed to produce a tonne of some common building materials.

Material	Energy (GJ)
Very high energy	
Aluminium	200–250
Plastics	50–100
Copper	100+
Stainless steel	100+
High energy	
Steel	30–60
Lead, zinc	25+
Glass	12–25
Plasterboard	8–10
Medium energy	
Lime	3–5
Clay bricks and tiles	2–7
Gypsum plaster	1–4
Concrete:	
in situ	0.8–1.5
blocks	0.8–3.5
precast	1.5–8
Sand lime bricks	0.8–1.2
Timber	0.1–5
Low energy	
Sand, aggregate	< 0.5
Flyash, RHA,	
volcanic ash	< 0.5
Soil	< 0.5

Floor foundations

The floor has to withstand the brunt of our fast, heavy and messy lifestyle. Yet good flooring really does act as a physical and decorative key, connecting rooms together and, when carefully chosen, helping us to maintain our homes as clean and healthy places.

THE SUBFLOOR

Underneath your floor is, for want of a better word, the subfloor. This flat surface supports the weight of you and your furniture and takes your choice of floor finish. In most homes, the subfloor will be made from either timber or concrete. These materials give your home different characteristics which can be exploited to your advantage. Before considering any further floor covering, however, check that the existing subfloor is sound (see chart opposite).

Concrete subfloors

These are generally found in modern buildings or in the basements of older homes and can be sealed, painted and waxed to provide easy-to-clean floor finishes in their own right. Most available concrete sealants are derived from petrochemicals and are not particularly ecofriendly, although the sheer simplicity of the sealant means that very little

> **for warm climates**
A polished concrete finish not only obviates the need for further floor coverings, but also looks stylish and feels cool under foot.

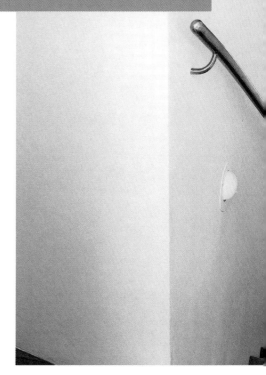

energy or material is wasted in its production. Concrete floors that are polished brick red are reminiscent of waxed earth floors found throughout Africa, while white painted concrete floors create a bright and thoroughly modern floor finish that can brighten darker rooms. To create a softer effect, lay down rugs.

The benefits of concrete subfloors are that they help homes in temperate climates to remain comfortable on hot or cold days because they absorb heat, spreading warmth into the night. They also provide sound insulation between floors and are easy to keep clean, provided that they are sealed. They require little more than a good sweep and the occasional mop, which makes them ideal for kitchens.

The downside is that they are not particularly comfortable to walk on and can make your home a noisy place, particularly if you have kids running around. They can be a source of damp in older homes and basements, and may

need to be sealed with waterproof rendering. They can also be treacherous when wet, even if painted with slip-resistant sealant.

Wooden subfloors

Timber joists form the basis for subfloors in most older homes and often in many new ones. The space between floor joists is commonly used to route water pipes and electrical cables, so consider future access before laying any further flooring on top. Timber floorboards are best sealed with ecofriendly natural waxes and oils to resist water marking and other stains. Natural wood stains come in a variety of colours, from white

spruce through to ebony, and also in a wide range of both opaque and translucent colours.

The benefits of timber subfloors are that they last for many years if properly cared for, remaining strong and resilient while ageing gracefully. Repairing existing softwood floorboards can also be a cheap way to improve your home. You can do this by taking up old wall-to-wall carpeting, removing any nails, mending creaking planks, then sanding and polishing with natural wax and oils.

The downside is that noise can easily travel through timber floors. However, this can be rectified by placing insulation material between the joists (the best eco-insulation is made from recycled paper that has been treated against fires and insects). Ideally the final floor finish should be separated from the joists by an insulating mat to create a floating floor.

Another potential problem is that timber joists might not be able to take the weight of additional heavy floor covering. If you have doubts, ask your flooring supplier to check the structural capacity of your existing floor.

Finally, timber floors will not last well in wet environments, so avoid them in bathrooms. They can be used in kitchens provided you are careful to clean up water spillages immediately.

While many environmental designers prefer the lightweight solution offered by timber floors, a ground bearing concrete slab does not use a great deal of energy but provides thermal mass, which helps to keep your home warm in winter and cooler in summer. Either way, insulate the ground floor by using expanded polystyrene under concrete floors and cellulose or mineral fibre insulation between the joists in timber floors (see page 38).

Upper floors, however are best made from timber joists because they are light and easy to install or modify. Concrete used for upper floors is heavy, requiring additional steel reinforcement, stronger supporting walls and deeper foundations, and is almost impossible to alter in the future.

SIGNS OF A SOUND SUBFLOOR

A good subfloor should exhibit the following key attributes:

Able to take existing and additional loads

If the floor gives under foot, call in a surveyor or structural engineer for advice.

Damp-proof

Danger signs of damp include smell, stains or soft-spots.

Well insulated

Old houses often have uninsulated ground floors which leak air and heat. Noise between floors can also be intrusive. These problems must be rectified before further work is carried out.

Flat and even

Uneven floors are often a sign of structural problems and make the addition of floor coverings more difficult.

Floor coverings

Whether you need a further floor covering over the subfloor depends not only on how you are going to use each room, but also on how you wish to live. Practical issues include cost, waterproofing, easy maintenance, noise reduction and safety. Colour and warmth, softness and comfort, and the ability to change with time are also considerations.

Whether you choose timber, stone, carpets, natural fibres or lino, ask your supplier for details to ensure that the material comes from a sustainable, ecofriendly source. The real environmental impact of flooring also comes after it is made, so check before buying that it can be maintained with ecofriendly cleaning products (see page 164, Chapter 6), it will age well and it can be reused, recycled or disposed of responsibly.

TIMBER

Wood can be the ultimate flooring material for your eco-home because it is naturally renewable, long-lasting, attractive, healthy and can be grown locally. Forests also provide habitats for most of the earth's plants and animals, create oxygen, store water and carbon, are home to some of the oldest human communities and give us some of the world's most stunning landscapes. Forests are also a source of natural medicines,

an economic resource for those who live in less industrialised societies and a critical part of our planet's climatic regulation.

Timber comes in many forms, ranging from thick planks of American red oak and Scandinavian birch ply panels to rich teak Thai parquet and cork tiles from the bark of Portuguese

> ### smooth and sleek
Not only is wood flooring an attractive, ecofriendly option, it is also warm under-foot and easy to clean. Lighter-coloured woods, such as maple, beech and birch, reflect sunlight, brightening the room.

oaks. While these are examples of timber from well-managed sources, very few of the hundred plus varieties sold across the world are grown and replaced carefully. Green guides to eco-timbers exclude all but three tropical hardwoods – teak, rubberwood and greenheart – of which only the hardwearing teak is suitable for flooring. Even then, very few teak plantations are managed well, so choose carefully.

When selecting timber, it is often best to choose woods grown in the temperate world. Since Europe has the most well-established woodland conservation programme, timber from Europe is a good bet, although careful forest management is now spreading worldwide. The most credible wood labelling programme was set up by the Forest Stewardship Council (FSC), a global organisation that ensures not only that wood sources are continuously replenished, but also that the rights of the local people and workers are protected. It further aims to complement natural forests by retaining old growth wilderness and conserving biodiversity. Look for the FSC logo when choosing your timber.

The right type of wood

Timbers are divided botanically. Softwoods are produced by coniferous trees, such as pines, while hardwoods are produced by broad-leaved trees, such as oak. Unfortunately, some hardwoods are soft and some softwoods are hard! Timber floors need to be durable and woods used in wet or humid environments need to be rot-resistant. Temperate hardwoods suitable for flooring range from pale birch and beech, to darker woods such as jarrah, oak and chestnut. Softwood flooring like fir, pine and European redwood are often faster growing and cheaper. Better still, choose reclaimed (that is, secondhand) timber, which is beautiful, seasoned and full of character, making it a very good eco-choice. Salvage and reclamation yards are plentiful and often have a wide range of interesting reclaimed woods at good prices.

Wood panel systems

Solid wood floors can be expensive, so many people choose composite timber panels, such as plywood, chipboard and MDF (medium density fibreboard), as cheap alternatives. Most of these panels are made from waste wood chippings which, in principle, is an environmentally sound process. In practice, however, the source of the wood may not be sustainable. Also, many panels are bonded together with chemical resins which are definitely toxic and have been linked to allergies. This is not to say that all board products are dangerous. Plywood

∧ **parquet perfection**
Traditionally laid by skilled craftspeople, parquet flooring is very stylish, hard-wearing and long-lasting.

ECOTIP

Protecting wooden floors
Waxes and varnishes will protect most woods from staining and damage. Beeswax protects most internal woods, but you can also buy solid oil varnishes, which are low in solvents and contain a variety of natural raw materials, such as linseed, sunflower, soybean and thistle oil, together with plant waxes. Internal woods don't need preservative treatment, many of which are harmful, but do need water protection. Wood also needs plenty of air circulating around it to prevent moisture from building up and causing rot. Avoid synthetic varnishes, such as polyurethanes, as these can cause skin irritation or allergic reactions.

∧ all floored

There is a huge variety of floor coverings for your home, each with their own merits and shortcomings. These include (clockwise from top left) carpets, stone tiles, rugs and Ttura, a type of terrazzo. When deciding which one to opt for, consider its suitability to the function of the room in question.

is probably the least toxic board material available and also the most attractive. Make sure that it comes from a truly sustainable source (in Europe, choose the White Swan nordic eco-label) and that the level of formaldehyde, a toxic resin used in the manufacture of wood panels, is listed as 'low' on the label.

HEAVY MATERIALS

Full of ecological contradictions, heavy flooring options are often misunderstood and misused. From a positive point of view, we will never run out of stone, sand, clay and gravel. Also, floors made from these materials need next to no maintenance over their long life because they are easy to clean and

hypo-allergenic. In warm climates, a shaded and well-ventilated room with stone or concrete floors will remain cooler in the heat of the day, while in cold climates, a heavy floor placed to catch the low winter sun will retain its heat long after night has settled in.

Yet floors made from stone, concrete or ceramics do consume considerable energy in their manufacture. Open-cast quarries degrade the landscape and often provide poorly paid and dangerous work. Transporting and machining heavy stone consumes vast quantities of fuel, as does firing cement and clay to make concrete and tiles. Heavy flooring may also entail making some structural modifications (such as larger foundations) to your home. Finally, concrete is considered the devil incarnate by some, with the vast majority of concrete buildings constructed in the last 50 years being ugly, dehumanising and often technically flawed.

To really benefit from these materials, you need to use them selectively. Restrict them to certain areas of the home such as the ground floor, where they will not be too heavy. They are also good for highly trafficked areas such as thresholds, hearth-stones, around the kitchen work triangle, and can also provide a waterproof surface in bathrooms. If used in a ventilated larder, food will be kept naturally cooler.

Stone

Ranging from smooth marble to rough hewn granite, stone is usually laid on a layer of cement on a concrete subfloor. Choose local stones that are in plentiful supply, from quarries that have strong environmental policies. These stones will not only be more ecological, they will also enhance your region's character and provide local employment. In the UK, for example, Welsh slate and limestone from the Cotswolds are better choices than Italian marble or cheaper South American slates.

Ceramics

Made from fired clay, ceramic tiles do cause environmental pollution even though the raw material is fairly unlimited. Tiles that contain recycled glass are more ecological. Ceramic floors are best restricted to areas where waterproof surfaces are helpful, such as in bathrooms or around kitchen sinks. Ceramic tiles are hard to fix to wooden subfloors as they do not expand and contract at the same rate as the timber underneath; in these instances, choose flexible flooring instead, such as linoleum or

rubber. Also, avoid glass and polished tiles on floors because they are very slippery when wet.

Tiles are regionally specific, despite worldwide marketing from manufacturers. Try to choose local tiles from small workshops that create beautiful objects with depth, texture and individual colour.

Terrazzo

This hard-wearing and waterproof flooring material is made from cement, sand and stone or glass chippings. Available either in tile form or poured and polished on site, terrazzo lasts indefinitely and can be polished to a very elegant sheen year after year. Some forms of terrazzo are made with an epoxy resin in place of cement. One such material, marketed as Ttura, is particularly ecofriendly, being made from 85 per cent recycled glass and non-solvinated epoxy resins.

> **encouraging warmth**
Laying down stone floors in the conservatory or another room that gets plenty of sun has the benefit of storing warmth for the whole house, which will also help to reduce your heating bills.

Brick

Hard-wearing but difficult to keep clean, brick floors are best used in areas that don't need to be kept spotless, such as hallways and work rooms. The manufacture of bricks is more energy-consuming than concrete products, so it's best to make use of reclaimed stock, which can be bought from salvage yards in many colours, ranging from rich browns to hard blues.

CARPETS AND RUGS

Fabric floor coverings have been made for many thousands of years and, although now ubiquitous, were once considered a luxury. Woven by hand with threads coloured by carefully chosen natural dyes, they were lain over earth, timber or stone floors to provide warmth, comfort and enchantment. Over the centuries, each local region developed its own style, sometimes abstract, sometimes figurative. The invention of the automated loom created a revolution in the production of textiles, and a carpet which might have been made in a week can now be woven in hours or less. The automated loom's insatiable demand for raw materials has led to the worldwide market for wool and cotton and the development of artificial fibres such as nylon and acrylic. It has also created one-dimensional products with no sign of human contact, each knot identical, and each colour completely uniform and consistent.

If you have a choice, rugs are a better eco-option for your home than fitted carpets. Rugs can be taken outside to be aired and beaten, removing the need for continuous vacuum cleaning and reducing the problem of house dust mites and other allergens. They can also be taken with you when you move home.

Fitted carpets, on the other hand, run under furniture, making them far harder to clean. They also require specialist equipment such as carpet shampoos. Although they appear to provide a flexible answer to modern furniture layout, the truth is that areas in the sun will eventually change colour. Well-trodden areas will lose their pile quickly and carpets placed under heavy furniture will eventually compress, requiring early replacement. Furthermore, carpets and their underlay give off polluting gases and the carpet fibres can trap toxins brought in from the street.

Ensuring that your carpeting has felt underlay made from recycled fabrics or wool sources with hessian backing, and not the more >

Eternally yours: rugs

Small, brightly coloured rugs on a timber floor are a far better ecological option than wall-to-wall fitted carpets. Not only are they easy to clean and provide warmth and comfort, they also age with us and are easy to take when we move home. Choose well-made wool, silk or cotton rugs that have been coloured with natural dyes.

Tatami mats

Filled with densely packed straw and covered with a
thin layer of more finely woven matting, rice straw slabs
are the key ingredient in traditional Japanese flooring.
Tatami mats are between 5 and 7cm (2–2¾in) thick and slightly under 1m (3¼ft) in
width and 2m (6½ft) in length. They are edged along the long sides with narrow
strips of black linen and lain in an anticlockwise spiral from the centre of a room. The
mat forms the basic unit around which rooms and homes were built – 8 mats for the
living space and 6 mats for the dining room. In Japan today, studio and apartment
dimensions are still described by the number of tatami mats they contain. The
covering layer should be replaced every three or four years. If you choose tatami mats
for part of your home, try to make it a shoe-free zone, as they are not hard-wearing.

> toxic polyurethane or rubber underlay, is a more ecofriendly gesture. Even so, many carpets are chemically treated to reduce staining and water damage, which can cause allergic reactions. If you opt for fitted carpets, introduce a 'no-shoes' policy in your home, air rooms once a week and vacuum regularly to remove bugs and dust.

The best textiles

The best fibres for floor coverings are natural ones like wool, cotton and silk. Wool carpets are usually made from sheep's wool which is soft, springy and long-lasting. It is a texture that holds dye well and provides warmth and good sound insulation. Even so, the wool industry does cause some pollution due to the chemicals used in sheep dips, the dyes used to colour the products and the fire retardants used to treat them.

Cotton rugs, such as kilims from Turkey, provide a lighter alternative to wool rugs. They are not as tough or long-lasting, however, and are best used in areas that are subject to less wear, such as bedrooms. They are good to have in bathrooms because they can soak up any water spillages on the floor, and then be hung outside to dry.

Silk is produced by the silk worm, which lives in China and feeds exclusively on mulberry leaves. These worms are farmed and killed in their millions for the fine, soft and exceedingly strong thread that is then dyed and woven to create tightly knotted and very soft carpets. Since the knots are extremely small, silk carpets are very long-lasting but expensive, and are best used as a small decoration rather than a wall-to-wall luxury.

Synthetic carpets are not as soft, durable or as environmentally sound as wool carpets, but they are cheaper. Nylon, polypropylene and acrylics are the most extensively used synthetics, and although they are available in a huge range of colours and styles, I do not recommend them. Nylon, for example, is responsible for the release of the greenhouse gas, nitrous oxide, which also contributes to ozone depletion and forms acid rain. Synthetic carpets are made from a variety of petro-chemically derived fibres that use high energy processes and produce many toxins over their life.

OTHER NATURAL FIBRES

The range of natural fibres available for flooring has grown

> **naturally trendy**
Natural fabrics such as (top to bottom) sisal, seagrass, coir and jute, have become very popular in recent times. Although they are attractive and have good eco-credentials, they are not very long-lasting and suffer from water damage and general wear and tear.

enormously in recent years as we have realised the enormous benefits of simple, biodegradable and healthy materials.

While each natural fibre has its own particular quality, they are all generally suitable for less trafficked areas but should be used with a no-shoes policy as they are particularly hard to keep clean. They are all quite abrasive under foot and you may wish to avoid them if you have small children.

Seagrass

Grown in seawater paddy fields in China, seagrass forms part of nature's tidal defenses, protecting and enhancing mangrove swamps and reefs. It is handwoven in a variety of decorative patterns and is naturally stain resistant (which also means that it can't be dyed). Modern and muted, seagrass is a popular choice in many homes, but bear in mind that it isn't a suitable material for stairs where it can become slippery under foot.

Hemp

Made from the cannabis plant, this has been used for a whole range of natural products. The earliest known use was in Southeast Asia over 6000 years ago and until the middle of the last century it was considered a great low-cost crop with thousands of applications ranging from fabrics and sealants to wall insulation. Anti-marijuana legislation stopped most

commercial production and it is only recently that hemp based products, including floor matting, have been reintroduced. Some people believe that the widespread use of hemp could dramatically reduce the use of other, more toxic, alternatives.

Coir

A waste product from coconut farming, coir is made from the nut's outer husk, which is first softened for up to a year in lagoons and then woven to produce a very hard-wearing mat. Popularly used outside the front door, it is also suitable indoors throughout the home. Although it

is basically a good green product, some of the estuaries have been polluted by the sheer volume of matting left to soften in them and this has adversely affected the local aquatic life.

Sisal

Grown from the grass stems of the sisalana bush in Africa and South America, this material is soft enough for bedrooms and tough enough to withstand chair legs in living and dining rooms.

Bamboo

This is the fastest growing plant on the earth. Resin-impregnated bamboo floorboards are tough,

v **simple and chic**
More practical than fitted carpet, sisal is a good choice for your dining room. The strong weave means that it won't decompress under the weight of seated diners.

easy to clean and available in a variety of widths and stains to suit living rooms and kitchens alike.

Jute

Long-stem plants around the Ganges Delta in Bangladesh provide the raw material for jute. It is mainly used in the production of hessian, but it is also available as a soft (and consequently short-lived) weave.

LINO, RUBBER AND SYNTHETICS

Resilient and smooth floor coverings are relatively modern and the cheapest means of providing a waterproof and easily cleaned surface. The most common smooth flooring is vinyl tiles or sheets. These are available in any colour, easy to fix, often designed to mimic natural floorings and are very cheap. Unfortunately they are manufactured from polyvinyl chloride (PVC), combined with fungicides, pigments and plasticisers, so are not the most ecofriendly of materials.

Linoleum is equally inexpensive as vinyl, but lasts longer and has better eco-credentials. It is made from mainly renewable and natural ingredients, chiefly linseed oil and natural resins mixed with cork, ground stone powder and wood flour, which are heat-bound onto a hessian backing. Not only are the resulting lino tiles safe, they have also been shown to kill harmful bacteria. Having said this, the raw materials often need to be transported a very long distance to reach their place of manufacture.

Many linoleum products are sold with a marbled effect slightly reminiscent of school corridors. There is a growing range of single colour tiles, however, that is much more modern. Always remember to use the natural adhesive called lignin paste to stick lino tiles down onto the floor rather than more toxic solvent-based glues.

Rubber is an alternative resilient material that is long-lasting and relatively benign. It does not contain plasticisers or heavy metals and one manufacturer claims that all their ingredients are eco-compatible and non-toxic.

Most rubber floors are made from artificial rubber with minimal natural latex. They are available in a wide range of colours and textures, but the flat and plain options are easier to clean and will last through more fashion changes than the dimpled, exotically coloured alternatives.

< alternative style
Modern designs have elevated the no-nonsense practical lino tile into a stylish, yet ecofriendly flooring option.

Internal walls

There are more walls than any other surface in a home – four in each room, two sides to each wall, inside and outside walls, loadbearing walls, window walls and stud partitions. Walls frame spaces, set limits to change, reflect and diffuse light, provide colour, hide wiring, and carry doors, windows and shelving. Sometimes we wish there were more walls in our home to create a playroom, study or second lavatory. At other times we crave more space and fewer rooms. Adding and removing walls is not a simple undertaking, but it is far easier than moving house, and it will certainly rejuvenate your home.

LOADBEARING WALLS

Made from brick or concrete, these create solid barriers between rooms and often support the floor above. They are hard to move but, like concrete floors, provide solidity, thermal stability and good acoustic separation between the spaces in your home.

Solid walls make electrical modifications hard work because routes for conduits need to be chased out and re-rendered. Also, they should never be removed without the advice of a builder or engineer since they might be supporting the floor above!

∧ the rough and the smooth

A couple of coats of paint will immediately transform a bare brick wall. Alternatively, you can render it with plaster to create a smoother surface that can be decorated with a wall finish of your choice or simply left bare.

STUDWORK WALLS

These are made from vertical and horizontal timber elements braced by floors and external walls. The timbers are covered with plasterboard panels and the space between the boards is used to run electrical cables and stuffed with sound absorbing insulation. They use far less material than load-bearing walls and are easier to modify for new wiring or new doors. Some studwalls do support floors above so, just as with solid walls, it is always best to check with a builder or engineer before you undertake to remove them.

If you are building new internal walls, then studwork provides the quickest, most flexible solution. Instead of building thin studwalls, consider constructing each wall as a wide storage space which can be accessed from either side and modified to suit your changing needs. Always check with your local authority first to see whether you need permission to build or remove walls.

WALL COVERINGS

Once you have a clean and flat wall, you can then decide how to decorate it. The typical considerations are colour and feel, maintenance and wear resistance. However, you should also consider how the walls will reflect and spread light, how their colour affects the warmth and size of rooms and how walls fit into other finishes, artworks and furniture in your home.

Ecofriendly paints

One of the cheapest and quickest ways to transform a room is to paint its walls a new colour. But walls do not stand alone from the rest of your furniture and finishes, and it is always best to be as careful in your choice of paint as you are in your choice of other home furnishings.

The chief differences between the various paints are their toxicity, durability, colour and sheen. Perhaps it's not surprising, but most of us spend far too much time agonising over the colour and far too little wondering about its effect on our health. The majority of paints available today are derived from the petrochemical industry, using synthetic dyes for

---

TECHNOLOGY

Studwork walls

Made from light timber frames, studwork walls are often used in modern houses and conversions.

Much easier and cheaper to build than the more solid brick walls, their eco-credentials can be maximised by filling the space between the two panels with mineral fibre or cellulose insulation material to increase the thermal and acoustic separation between rooms. You can also build storage spaces into studwork walls, creating thick walls that make a pleasant transition between spaces.

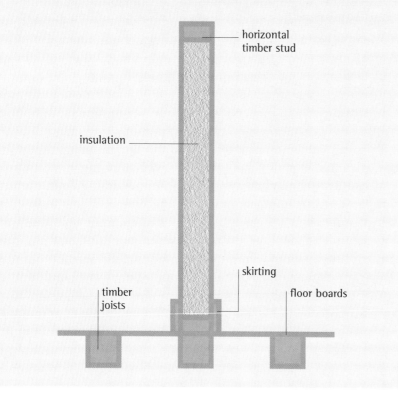

horizontal timber stud

insulation

skirting

floor boards

timber joists

colour and a rich and toxic mix of solvents, binders, emulsifiers, fillers, thinners and drying agents. Small wonder that painting is officially recognised as a dangerous and unhealthy trade.

Synthetic paints

If you do use these, avoid high-sheen water-based paints and all solvent-based paints inside the home, as they give off high levels of toxic volatile compounds. Low-sheen water-based paints are still toxic but emit less than a fifth of the chemicals associated with other synthetics. In all cases, ensure that the room you are painting is well ventilated and that any doors between this room and the rest of your home are closed. Don't use the room until the paint is completely dry and all traces of odour are gone. Paints are now being labelled with health warnings that indicate the amount of volatile organic compounds (VOC) they contain, so read the label carefully to ensure that VOC levels are low. Better still, choose natural paints that only contain healthy ingredients, such as chalk, linseed oil, earth pigments, beeswax, talcum powder and harvested tree resins.

Plant-based paints, waxes and varnishes

These are available in a wide range of colours and textures from specialist shops, some mainstream

CLOSE-UP: PAINT PIGMENTS

Some paints can be purchased without added colour so that you can create your own hues from natural pigments. Earth pigments include oxides of iron (which are red to brown), ochres, umbers and greys. Richer colours can be obtained from mineral pigments extracted from the ground, cleaned and milled. Some of these are also heat-treated to create different colours. You can mix pigments together if you can't find the colour you like, but be aware that these natural pigments are not generally as intense as commercial dyes. Certain ranges consist of more intense pigments derived from the chemical industry. These aren't so ecofriendly as the natural ones but, all things considered, don't rule out a brightly coloured wall if you think it'll look great in your home!

DIY stores or direct from the manufacturers. They are suitable for internal and external painting on plaster, timber and metal surfaces and have minimal health hazards. Some natural paints take longer to dry than synthetic ones, but they are less toxic so the rooms can be used straight after painting. Plant-based paints are also microporous, which means that although they are water-resistant, they still allow water vapour to flow through the wall, which helps to prevent the paint from blistering.

> **design tools**
Once you've got the knack, wallpaper is relatively simple to hang and will mask minor bumps and holes in wall surfaces.

Alternative indoor paints

Distemper is a traditional paint made from chalk and linseed oil binder. It can be wiped clean but isn't suitable in areas that will be easily marked, such as in children's bedrooms or hallways.

Casein paints are made from distemper bound with a milk by-product. The casein helps to bind and seal the paint, making it washable and longer-lasting.

Wall surfaces can also be given depth and texture by using fine clay render or adding mineral powder to the paint mixture. Natural paints are often provided in powder form for mixing with water at your home. Natural resin emulsion paints look and behave just like commercial emulsions but don't contain harmful ingredients.

If you are decorating outside walls or directly onto plaster or cement, then you can use mineral paints which are manufactured from waterglass (potassium silicate) and inorganic colour pigments. This type of paint actually binds deep into the cement base to create a coloured surface which is durable, colourfast and easily cleaned. It is odourless, non-toxic and allows the wall to breathe. Potassium silicate can also be used directly with water to prime loose and dusty wall surfaces or can be mixed with natural pigments to create a colour wash glaze.

Wallpaper

Covering walls with printed paper provides instant colour, texture, pattern, and a wipe-clean surface. Wallpapers range from thick lining papers designed to cover uneven walls through to highly decorated, hand-finished patterns and mass-produced textured vinyl.

Wallpaper is a good environmental material as its chief ingredient is wood pulp, which is either grown in a sustainable manner or comes from recycled sources. You also need only a small amount of wallpaper to cover a wall. The print dyes found in wallpaper generally come from the chemical industry, but it is possible to find some wallpapers hand-printed with natural dyes. Alternatively, you can simply buy plain lining and decorate it yourself with natural paints. Wallpaper also has the advantage of providing a quick way to hide an uneven wall surface.

Paper is used as the backing for a variety of natural materials, including cork, hessian and raffia, that can be hung on walls. The paper makes it easier to hang these materials, which you can mix and match to create changing textures and colours on one wall.

It is also possible to purchase vinyl wallpaper, which is basically paper covered in a thin film of pvc. This type of wallpaper is often used in wet environments, such as bathrooms and utility rooms because it is not damaged by water and can be easily wiped clean. While the amount of vinyl used is relatively small, the ideal eco-home should not have it, not least because vinyl and textured paper is one of the most unattractive finishes imaginable!

Wood panelling

Walls that are wood-panelled provide a soft and warm alternative to other types of wall coverings. Use tongue and groove solid wood panels and treat them with natural waxes, oils or coloured varnishes. Vary the look by hanging strips vertically or horizontally or by choosing wide planks instead of the usual narrow boards. Alternatively, use large plywood panels to create a modern wall that can incorporate hidden light fittings and storage space in a smooth and semi-reflective surface. As wood panelling doesn't take heavy loads and water damage is unlikely, choose softer woods like pine, as these are a good and cheap choice. You can also use cork tiles for additional heat and noise insulation.

Tiles

Made from fired clay or glass, tiles come in all sizes, colours and prices, and are a long-lasting, maintenance free and water resistant option for covering your walls. Small tiles are now sold on backing sheets of hessian or paper, allowing you to fix large

quantities quickly and accurately. Ceramic tiles are opaque and are usually glazed for protection. Unglazed tiles need to be waxed like timber and will age gently over time. Glass tiles add sparkle to wall finishes and are generally more expensive. Tiles can be laid in a huge number of imaginative

∧ wall to wall
The huge array of wall coverings leaves you spoilt for choice when decorating your home. They include (clockwise from top left) large stone tiles, painted wooden tongue and groove, metal wall finishes and mosaic ceramic tiles.

∧ glass bricks
Create an internal wall or partition using glass bricks. Use them sparingly to lighten rooms that have poor access to natural light.

∧ walls to bounce off
Rubber sheets can also be used on walls. They make a tough, long-lasting alternative to ceramics, particularly in rooms that get wet.

patterns. They are best used in wet environments, around baths and showers and in kitchens, but work equally well on vertical and horizontal surfaces.

Tiles consume more energy and materials in their manufacture than paper or paint, so it is best to limit their use to areas that will benefit from water resistance.

Metal wall finishes

Walls of aluminium, stainless steel or copper sheeting have recently become fashionable, and although these are considered 'minimal' in the world of interior design, they are actually 'maximal' (if that's a word) in ecological terms. To produce aluminium, for example, tonnes of bauxite need to be dug out from the side of a mountain, a whole region has to be flooded to build a hydro-electric dam and the resulting sheets of metal then need to be shipped across the world.

If you must have metal wall finishes, limit them to small areas of your home and use stainless steel in preference to other metals. Consider installing a small square of beaten polished copper plate in the centre of an unplastered wall so the reflecting copper becomes a shimmering piece of art instead of an expensive and environmentally destructive decorative foil.

External
materials

Few of us have the opportunity to construct our homes from scratch, but maybe once in our lives, we are lucky enough to build an extension or convert the attic.

THE ROOF

Possibly the most critical part of the home, the roof protects the rest of your home from the worst of the weather and potentially

enables you to collect natural resources for reuse. If you are moving to a new house, look for pitched or sloping roofs as these shed rain quickly and are easier to maintain than flat roofs. Flat roofs also have to take the load of snow so are not advisable if you live in a cold climate. You also need to consider the use of the space underneath the roof. In places

where land is at a premium, a loft makes inexpensive real estate, so aim to design the roof structure for living space rather than storage. Avoid closely spaced gang-nail trusses, which are cheaper but fill the attic space with structure, and choose wider timber beams and rafters supported on vertical columns instead. Placing insulation directly under the roof plane between joists will ensure that the roof space is ready for occupation when you need it.

On pitched roofs, timber shingles or thatch are the most benign covering as they require little energy to make. However, there are few regions in the industrialised world where these sorts of roofs are commonly used and they do require careful maintenance. Concrete tiles use less energy than traditional clay or slate tiles but they are still being made to mimic other materials rather than expressing their own nature, which seems a shame. Of the metal roofing options, only

< green tops

If you're building or repairing a flat roof, consider a turf covering. As well as being attractive and self-maintaining, it will also provide a home for birds.

recycled stainless steel sheeting offers a low energy, low maintenance and non-toxic roof covering. If you opt for metal roofing, avoid lead, copper and zinc as these cause damage to water-borne animals.

If your home has a flat roof or you are planning to design a flat roof for an extension, it should ideally be made from softwood joists and panels because these are low energy renewable materials. Consider covering it in a shallow layer of earth in which you can plant grasses. This provides an alternative sunbathing terrace and will attract birds, insects and other flora and fauna found in a conventional garden. To make the roof waterproof, use an EPDM elastomeric sheeting and cork or expanded polystyrene for insulation under the earth layer. Slope the roof by an angle of more than three degrees in order to avoid water building up on the roof surface.

WINDOWS

Single glazed windows are good at letting light in but they also let heat out. It is therefore essential that you choose double glazed window units and you'll save even more energy if you install low-e double glazing or triple glazing, particularly if you live in a cool climate. A typical home needs no more than 20 to 30 per cent of its wall surface glazed in order to be brightly lit by the sun during the day and to keep in its heat at night. Use larger windows on sun-facing walls and smaller ones on shady façades.

Timber window frames protected with plant based paints are twice the price of PVC window frames, but are more beautiful and, properly maintained, last longer. An even better option is to choose water resistant wood for the frames, such as tough European oak and hemlock. Overhanging eaves will also protect windows from driving rain. Metal frames made from steel or aluminium need more energy to construct than timber windows, but are easier to maintain. No matter what material you decide on for your window frames, they all need to be repainted or protected after the first five or ten years.

< style and function
Bathrooms built by an exterior wall allow for natural ventilation. Opaque glass replaces paper tiles in this distinctly Japanese-style bathroom, allowing the wall to serve as a window, too.

> murcatt's eco-home

The Australian architect, Glen Murcatt, has designed a home made from steel, glass and wood, which is appropriately sited around natural bushland in Sydney.

Another element to consider in your choice of window is how it opens. Side hung windows are easy to open and close to a tight seal in winter, while sash windows are more prone to failure. Avoid top or centre-hung windows as these will provide only a small opening in summer or intrude in the room when open fully.

If you live in a warm climate, choose inward opening or sash windows so that you can close external louvres for shade and security on hot days, but maintain a cooling breeze.

DOORS

Like windows, doors should provide an air-tight seal for comfort during winter. The best designs incorporate draught-proofing and are made with insulated timber panelling or low-e double glazed windows.

EXTERNAL WALLS

The cost of a timber framed home is similar to a brick home and both last for an equally long time if properly detailed.

An interesting alternative to timber framing is constructing an extension to your home from a frame that is made of recycled steel, which is then protected in stainless steel profiled cladding (again, recycled). This system is commonly used for industrial warehouses, but a good architect might be able to create something quite special on a domestic scale.

The reason for its good eco-credentials is the fact that a timber cladding system will need maintenance and repair every five to ten years, whereas stainless steel cladding will need very little.

The final key to an ecologically sensitive wall is the generous use of insulation as discussed in Chapter 2. Choose cellulose fibre for a timber frame and rock or glass wool for a loadbearing cavity wall and ensure that you use at least 150mm (6 inches), if not more, to keep your home cosy through the cold winter nights and cool during summer days.

Furnishings and fittings

It is only when we move home and the delivery van slowly fills with sofas, tables, lamp-stands and bookcases that we realise how many possessions we have accumulated over the years. At times like these we may find ourselves wondering how we ever decided to buy that coffee table, cushion or whatnot. Often the reasons are clouded in time, but the truth is that we are easily persuaded by instant appeal and cost. We are never really given much information about where it comes from, what it is made out of or how long it will last.

∧ multi-functional
Try to choose furniture that has dual purposes, as well as being made from sustainable resources. A futon sofa, for example, transforms into a spare bed.

Some companies are beginning to make a move in the right direction but there is no clear guide to whether the furniture we choose is environmentally friendly.

One way to assess for this is by thinking in the long-term before you buy. Imagine whether you will still like it in twenty years' time. Check, too, that it is well-made so that it will actually last this long. If there is no manufacturer information on testing, then sit on furniture and lift it up to see if it's been designed for the real world. Ask the retailer what it is made from and where it was manufactured. If you have a choice, go for low energy or recycled goods that are made locally over high energy foreign imports. Consider multi-functional, adaptable and portable furniture that you can use in a variety of ways as time goes by.

While wood is usually a good bet, don't forget that recycled glass and metal are often beautiful objects in themselves. You should also accept that plastic, for all its faults, is a material that can be transformed into cheap, long-lasting and funky products, provided that designers and manufacturers understand and respect its qualities of lightness, strength and translucency.

suits you
Whether you prefer a country-house style (above) or a modern, more minimalist look (right), an ecofriendly home is one that allows you to express your individual tastes.

WOOD FURNITURE

If you're contemplating purchasing tables and chairs, the likelihood is that you are probably looking at wood, whether you are more interested in a traditional style with well-turned legs and inlaid veneers, or a more modern design.

People tend to spend a lot of time and money choosing wooden furniture, yet how many stop to think where the wood comes from

and what might have become of its forest home and the wildlife? The same basic guidelines apply to buying wooden furniture as to choosing timber for flooring and other decorative purposes, although wood used for furniture is generally either exposed and hard-wearing or hidden, low-grade and simple.

Solid wood furniture can be a delight, ageing well and travelling with you through your life. Make sure that the wood is sourced from sustainable forests and avoid delicate frames or thin veneers which are easily broken. Once you have made your purchase, treat the wood with care, waxing it regularly and wiping off water stains as quickly as you can. If you have the choice, choose solid wood over a wood veneer because a wood surface can always be resanded and finished should it deteriorate, while veneers are very hard to replace.

Low-grade timber is often used to frame sofas and beds. The problem with this wood is not that it comes from fast-disappearing native forests, but that it is designed for a short life and often contains mildly toxic chemicals.

When choosing sofas and other covered furnishings, always lift up the skirt and have a good look at the timber and joints underneath. Wooden furniture should be held together with strong timber joints or good metal brackets and bolts, rather than staples and glue. Poor quality furniture often looks fine when first put up, but it can easily be damaged when you start to move it around at home. Choose solid woods or plywood in preference to chipboard covered with melamine or veneers (look for the Forestry Stewardship Council mark on labels). If you do use chipboard, always choose those with a low formaldehyde content as they will not pollute your home. For more information on pollutants found in the home, see page 165, Chapter 6.

METALS

Although beautiful, long-lasting and relatively easy to recycle, metals are also rare, often toxic and require intensive energy to extract. According to the World Resource Institute, we will run out of mineable metals in less than 100 years, with the exceptions of nickel, iron and aluminium. What's more, the energy required to mine 1 kg (2.2 lbs) of iron is 30 times greater than the energy required to harvest 1 kg (2.2 lbs) of wood: and aluminium requires 100 times as much energy as wood! Natural habitats are often destroyed by the huge quantities of material that are moved to extract metal.

If you do choose to furnish your home with metals, you should think of these items as precious, treating them like jewellery for

your home. A general principle is to use wood for larger items and metal for smaller ones. Instead of covering your kitchen with stainless steel, for instance, use metal as a focal point in your design – a stunning candle holder or an elegant copper trim set into the top of a dark elm coffee table.

Aluminium

This very light and strong metal is extracted from bauxite ore in a process requiring huge inputs of electricity. Fortunately, much of this energy is created using hydro-

> iron everywhere

You may not realise it, but iron and its alloys have a place in every part of your home. (From top to bottom) Cast iron can be used to make coat hooks, galvanised steel is suitable for wall cabinets, brushed steel is used to make cooking vessels and chrome-plated steel makes a long-lasting hook for keys.

electric power, which is a renewable resource. Yet the resulting loss of natural habitat, toxic spoils and secondary emissions make excess use of aluminium a bad thing.

Aluminium can be used all over the home and, being lightweight and easy to store, has become a popular alternative for window frames, garden furniture, guttering and curved roofing. Since aluminium degrades in acidic rain, much of it is powder coated which makes recycling impossible. This is unfortunate because unadulterated aluminium is easy and cheap to reuse. Inside the home, aluminium retains a dull light grey sheen which is chic and modern. Instead of using aluminium panels to cover walls and floors, reserve it for detail – high quality iron-mongery, storage containers, picture frames and light fittings.

Copper

This soft, dull red-gold-coloured metal fades to green as it weathers. It is a high energy

METALS AND THEIR YEARS UNTIL EXHAUSTION

Once used for ornament and tools, metals are now regularly thrown away. If we use them in our homes, we should treat them like a piece of precious jewellery.

Metal ore	Years remaining
Gold	30
Silver	30
Lead	45
Zinc	50
Cadmium	50
Tin	55
Copper	60
Mercury	80
Nickel	120
Iron	230
Bauxite	260
Uranium	410
Manganese ore	685

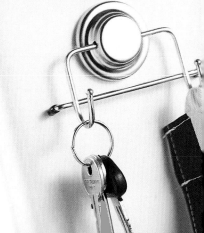

product with less than 100 years left in the ground and its extraction from mines causes huge levels of pollution. Over 50 per cent of copper is recycled because of its high resale value.

Hand-beaten copperware has been used and valued for thousands of years and makes highly conductive saucepans. As copper oxide is toxic, make sure you clean cookware made from this material very well. Copper is also used around the home for water pipes and roof-flashing, but because it is so scarce, it is better to use plastic or stainless steel for plumbing purposes and polyester or galvanised steel for guttering.

Iron and steel

The iron age heralded our transition from hunter/gatherers to farmers and communitarians. Closer to the present age, iron helped to create the industrial revolution, giving us the strength to build steam engines which then made bridges, sky-scrapers and automobiles. We are now recycling over 70 per cent of scrap iron and the energy content of iron and steel (which is an alloy of iron) is lower than other metals.

Steel and iron rust when used, so they are normally plated, enamelled, painted or galvanised to protect them from corrosion. All these processes are harmful and the steel industry is responsible for the release of hormone disrupting dioxins and other toxins. In the home, we often use stainless steel which is protected from corrosion by the addition of chromium. Traditional uses of steel include cutlery, kitchen equipment, worktops and bathroom panelling. Stainless steel is long lasting and easy to clean and recycle. It makes a good choice for things in your home that will get wet.

Lead

In the past this soft, dark grey metal was used for roofing and plumbing, but it should not be used anywhere in the home because of its known toxic effects. If you are considering using rainwater from the roof as your supply of drinking water, check that all lead flashings have been replaced. Old paint may also contain lead so if you are stripping any old paintwork be sure to wear a protective mask and long sleeves. Opening windows to create good ventilation and vacuuming afterwards are also good protective measures.

Eternally yours: cutlery

A set of stainless steel cutlery will last a lifetime, so consider your choice carefully. Because it is a very easy metal to work with, you will have lots of design options, ranging from the traditional to the modern. It is also lightweight, dishwasher-proof, and water and stain resistant. Compared to silver it is relatively cheap and has better eco-credentials.

Zinc

With less than 50 years of reserves, this is another metal that is near the end of its life.

Zinc is generally used for galvanising steel, but it has also found a niche as a fashionable finish for kitchen worktops in many modern homes. Since galvanised steel has a short life and the zinc coating is toxic to water-borne organisms, it is better to opt for stainless steel or a less energy-intensive material.

GLASS

Transparent or translucent, reflecting and refracting light, glass is like ice, frozen solid but still a liquid. It is made from sand, carbonates and sulphates, heated to mind-numbing temperatures of 1500°C (2730°F) and then blown, spun or floated to produce glassware, glass fibres and window panes. It can be used in the home for spreading and diffusing light, or as an object of beauty in itself.

Many pieces of glassware are made from recycled sources and you should choose these over more refined designs. Recycling glass reduces the need to extract more materials, reduces waste and cuts energy use by at least a tenth. Also, sea sand cannot be used for glass-making and the mining of silver sand continues to cause local environmental damage.

Glass can be easily recycled for most practical household uses, except for windows panes which need to be made from uncontaminated glass to retain their strength.

Once formed glass is non-toxic and air-tight, making it ideal for storing foods and drink.

PLASTIC

Plastics are mainly derived from the oil industry and make up around 5 per cent of the world's oil consumption. These materials are responsible for the release of large quantities of harmful toxins

∧ **the beauty of glass**

Glass and water have a natural affinity, each capturing and reflecting light in their own way. Recycled glass with natural flaws makes a perfect container for flowers on a sunny window ledge or it can be used more ambitiously and creatively, as is the case with this modern bathroom basin.

during their manufacture and are rarely recycled, resulting in growing mounds of useless and complex waste. Some plastics are relatively simple, requiring little energy to make, releasing little pollution during their manufacture and being very easy to recycle. Polyethylene and polypropylene fall into this camp.

Polypropylene has found its way into our homes as a tough storage container for food and also as a cheap material for making translucent mugs, waste bins and general storage.

Polyethylene is generally used to make thin films for wrapping and bags. It is rarely recycled so it is best to use thicker reusable carriers instead of thin throw away ones. Try not to base the design of your home around an extensive use of plastic. Rather, find small objects that fit into your general colour scheme and use them to complement a more natural surrounding.

PVC (the household name for polyvinyl chloride) is on the hit list for many environmental organisations. While it is a low-energy consumer (it is made from salt and petroleum), its main disadvantage is the highly toxic dioxins that are created during manufacture and incineration. It is also mixed with plasticisers and heavy metals which are known to be toxic. Manufacturers are struggling hard to prove that both

∧ poetic plastics

Many companies have discovered that simple plastics, such as polypropylene, make refined and long-lasting objects, such as chairs, storage containers and jugs. These good uses of plastics around the home should be encouraged.

the additives and PVC itself are harmless and better for the environment than natural alternatives. Environmentally, PVC can only really be justified in situations where it is long lasting, such as in underground pipes. Even then, other plastics are just as strong and most environmentalists would recommend ceramics instead.

Finally, and just as importantly, most PVC products found in the home, such as window frames and garden furniture, are rarely attractive and age rather badly. It is much better to save up for that little bit longer and buy something that really adds value, as well as beauty, to your home.

Other synthetics found in the home include bitumen sheets (which are used for flat roofing), melamine (used as a water-resistant coating for tables and worktops), EPDM elastomers (again used for flat-roofing and rubber seals), polyurethane (used in varnishes, sealants and in roof sheeting) and polystyrene (used for insulation and light-weight packing materials). Natural alternatives such as cork, timber and coconut fibres are better for the environment, but it will be hard to avoid some use of synthetics in your home. Try to limit their use, however, and ask suppliers for alternative materials where possible.

Fabrics and fillings

Cushions, curtains, pillows, duvets, mattress fillings and soft furniture all add colour, texture and bounce to our surroundings. Without them, rooms can feel hard and clinical.

When choosing fabrics and fillings, factors to consider are the pollution created by the dyes and how the different fibres affect your health. While fabrics are generally fairly innocuous, a little thought can go a long way in helping to keep the planet clean.

NATURAL FIBRES

These are long-lasting, non toxic and renewable materials which, when farmed well, contribute to healthy and vibrant country economies. Although sheep are dipped in harmful chemicals and cotton crops are sprayed with pesticides, natural materials still remain favourite fabrics for many green buyers because they breathe well, do not create static electricity and are relatively non-allergenic. Nevertheless, the cotton plant is one of the most polluting farming products on the planet, using 2 per cent of all farmland and consuming a quarter of all pesticides. And downstream of the cotton fields, huge quantities of synthetic dyes are used to colour our cotton and wool.

Cotton

This has many uses round the home, from napkins and table-cloths to bed sheets and towels. Some growers are not only reducing the need for pesticides, but they are also cross-breeding natural cottons to create a range of subtle colours from brown through mint green to pale pink, which need neither bleach, defoliants or dyes. If you can search out these cottons, you will be making a significant improvement to the environment. Look for organic labelling (Soil Association in the UK or Natural Cotton Colours – the US growers of natural Acala Pima and soft Sea Island long-staple cotton).

Linen

Derived from the straw of the flax plant, linen ranges from cream to dark tan and grey. It is a good eco-material being absorbent, colourfast and full of texture.

Wool

Wool products are heavier than other fabrics but are often longer lasting as well as better for the environment. Choose those materials that are naturally dyed and use them as throws or bedding to add warmth and colour to your home.

tactile sensation
As well as colour and style, the texture of fabrics you choose for your home will also add to the overall mood you are aiming to create in each room.

Leather

This material can be extremely long-lasting provided you choose a tough grade, it is properly stitched and used on well-made furniture. However, the inhumane methods of production, particularly the slaughterhouse, taint leather's green image. The tanning process is also highly toxic and includes treatment with solvents and chemicals such as chromium sulphate.

To care for leather, use natural waxes to replenish the skin and choose your leather furniture carefully so that you will treasure it for years to come. Avoid cheap leather suites that are not only poorly made but also exceedingly ugly to look at.

SYNTHETIC FIBRES

Nylon, polyester and acrylic are the most common synthetic fibres found around the house and are used for fillings as well as fabrics. Although generally hard wearing, they attract dust and do not breathe as well as natural fibres. Synthetic fibres cause less environmental damage than poorly grown cotton, but they are not as comfortable or as easy to clean. Renewable synthetics include rayon and acetate which are made from wood waste.

Synthetic fillings are easier to wash than feather ones and are a good alternative for people who are allergic to feathers. Latex

wildlife options
For a funkier look, try decorating a room with animal print fabrics. The real thing is very durable, but avoid endangered species and skins obtained through cruelty!

fillings (made from foam rubber) are also germ-resistant and washable, but they get hot in summer and can be sweaty.

Nylon was invented by the French manufacturer Dupont, along with teflon and lycra.

Originally it was used to replace silk in hosiery manufacture, but it is now used in a vast array of products. It is best used for outside furniture because it is water repellent and extremely strong.

Another new synthetic fibre that is very ecofriendly is tencel. Like viscose, this is derived from wood pulp, but does not use a chemical solvent. The resulting cloth, when mixed with cotton, is very strong, soft and colourfast.

NATURAL FILLINGS

No matter the quality of your fabric choice, it is the type and quality of the fillings that make or break upholstery and bedding.

ECOTIP

Choosing the right fabric
Fabrics produced in an environmentally friendly way include organic cotton, sheep's wool, hemp yarn and Tencel, a manmade fabric derived from wood pulp. Choose fabrics in their natural colours, then dye them with natural dyes. Cushions with removable covers make them easier to wash and darker coloured fabrics are best for sofas and chairs because they don't show up the dirt as much.

Down is the most expensive filling but always plumps itself up and never loses its springiness. Down from the eider duck is the warmest and much of it is collected during the moulting season rather than from the slaughter-house, making it an ethical and ecological filling. Use down in pillows, duvets and scatter cushions for extra comfort.

Duck and goose feathers are not as warm, soft or springy as down, and you'll need nearly three times as many for the equivalent cushion because they are very fine. They are, however, cheap and long-lasting. Some people have allergic reactions to feather, in which case synthetic fibres provide a healthy alternative.

SYNTHETIC FILLINGS

There is a very good selection of these. Both acrylic and polyester wadding are washable and hypo-allergenic but also need to be tightly packed into a rigid fabric casing in order to avoid becoming lumpy. Foam chips and blocks are cheap but not comfortable or long-lasting. They also need to be treated with fire-retardant chemicals to reduce the risk of catching alight. After

several years of wear, blocks do crumble and the resulting waste is neither biodegradable or reusable. Latex foam is made from natural rubber and lasts for longer than synthetic foam. It is especially good for using inside the parts of the sofa that you sit on, while the sofa backrest and cushions are best filled with feather and down.

< covers, curtains and throws
Fabrics are a cheap and easy way to decorate your home, so explore the options and aim to colour co-ordinate.

CLOSE-UP: UPHOLSTERY

Whether covered in leather or fabric, upholstered furniture was traditionally designed with a solid timber chassis, covered with horsehair and tied together with hessian and flax – all natural materials and all designed to last a long time. Modern and cheaper alternatives, such as those made from mdf, staples, foam and synthetic covers, may look similar in the showroom but will often wear badly, provide poor support and be hard to fix when damaged. When buying new upholstery ask for details on how the furniture has been constructed, what has been used for the fillings and how easy it is to clean and replace sections of fabric.

Rooms
for living

Each room in your home provides you with a protected space that should last for many years, grow with you and allow you to express yourself. Practical, beautiful, adaptable, harmonious, easy to clean and easy to live in, rooms should also conserve resources and help to improve the quality of our environment, both locally and globally. The American architect, Frank Lloyd Wright, said that a home should be woven like a rug so that it is tough, comfortable, beautiful and consistent. As we move from one room to the next, patterns and materials should repeat and hold the whole together. More than this, we should try to do more with less, remembering an old Japanese proverb, 'a home which keeps the rain out and has enough food to keep us from starving – this is sufficiency'.

Chapter Four

Entrances, halls and stairs

Few people consider corridors, staircases and the entrance way when assessing their home's eco-worthiness. Yet these secondary spaces are just as vital as the main rooms and, with some creative thought, hold a great deal of design potential.

THE ENTRANCE WAY

This transitional space is the way in and out of your home. It should have an inviting face, keep warm air in and cold air out, have enough space for waiting and unloading, and finally be a place to greet and say goodbye. In order to fulfil these activities, it needs to be designed in an overlapping and seamless way.

Since the entrance way is the most trafficked area of your home, avoid laying carpet as this wears easily. Instead, fit a large and tough coir mat and use hard flooring, such as stone or concrete covered with linoleum. Consider using a ceramic tile or panelled finish on the lower section of the wall to protect it from the frequent

> ### welcome home
Beyond a solid front door, every home needs a lobby where you can take off overcoats, store wet umbrellas, hang up hats, take off mucky shoes, drop your keys, put down mail and leave messages.

knocks caused by incoming bikes, prams and other household deliveries.

Keep the hallway relatively light in colour as this will help your eyes adjust between the bright outside and the darker interior. Ideally, install a window by the front door so you can see visitors and have natural light. To create soft lighting, connect the light switch by the door to desk lamps, rather than overhead fittings.

CORRIDORS AND STAIRS

Often considered a waste of space, it is possible to make these thoroughfares more productive by incorporating them into the living space. A single, large, multi-functional room in which to lounge, dine and entertain can stretch from the back to the front of your home. With windows on two sides, there will be an ever-changing play of natural light in this room, giving you the opportunity to vary its use.

Where corridors are needed for privacy or structural reasons, try to keep them as short as possible. Try to design them so they incorporate as much storage as possible. They should also have access to natural light, either from skylights above or by adding

< overview
In a two storey home, open plan living can also accommodate an open staircase, adding a third dimension to your house.

∧ **safety precautions**
All staircases should have banisters or railings, and any coverings should be non-slip. If you have children, avoid stairwells or steps with a steep gradient.

internal glazing between the corridor and adjacent living rooms

To prevent hallways from becoming blank, faceless and lifeless routes, hang lots of pictures or photos of family and friends along their walls. In larger homes, corridors and stairs may form part of a protected route in case of fire. Therefore, before making any major changes to these areas of your home, always check with an architect or surveyor who will advise you of any possible problems.

Corridors and stairs get the most wear in your home and therefore need tough finishes that will last well. Hard flooring and tiled walls are easy to keep clean while light colours will widen and brighten narrow spaces.

To save energy in hallways, reduce the temperature on your radiator thermostats there and use low energy lighting with timer switches which will turn off automatically after a minute or so.

stylish storage
A basket on the stairs (above) is one way to gather items and avoid running up and down constantly. Storage ideas for larger entrances include (right) extended coat rails, hooks, trolley baskets and high level or slimline shelves.

< versatility
If a corridor is wide enough, you can use it as extra study space. If you have to squeeze past a desk, however, then it really shouldn't be there.

Living rooms and lounging

Today's living rooms work hard for their keep and need to be quick-changing from relaxation to formality or from entertainment to work. Since so much of our time at home is spent here, we should put as much of ourselves into the space as possible.

LOCATION

The living room needs to occupy the most comfortable part of the home. It should be quiet and restful, have good views and enough space to cope with seating, informal eating, storage and idle loafing. Ideally, it should face the afternoon or evening sun, which may mean that the traditional 'front room' is totally inappropriate. Close to the garden and the kitchen, the main living space may need to take over the rear kitchen or even move upstairs so that it is overlooking the back garden with stairs leading directly outdoors. If this is not possible, then open up the front room to the back so that light and views spread across the full depth of the floor.

Living rooms also need to break outside when the weather is good. One ideal way of achieving this is by replacing an existing window with glazed french doors that you can open in the summer. This will also bring more light into the room and increase the connection between the indoors and outdoors, even when it is closed.

Better still, you will gain some more space by building a conservatory between the back garden and the living room. This way you will be able to capture a small part of the natural world and let it infiltrate your home for much of the year.

Another way of increasing the strength of your living room space is by opening it up to upper floors. This can be achieved either by incorporating the staircase within the living room or by breaking out part of the upper floor to create a double height space.

SUITABLE FLOORING

Living rooms need to be comfortable and relaxing, and lounging on the floor is just as

> minimalism

This living room is neither cluttered by furniture nor confused by colour. Each item sits alone with enough space to breathe, yet everything has a unity.

> material options

The ultimate eco-living room is one filled with natural fabrics, including wooden floorboards, leather chairs, muslin blinds and paper lanterns.

> storage ideas

Wood tables and wicker consoles are easy and cheap to put together, and are far less taxing ecologically than the more common glass and steel cabinets.

important as sitting on a comfortable chair. Timber floors are fine, provided there are plenty of rugs and cushions, as this allows your guests the option of relaxing at floor level as well. A concrete floor is cold in winter, but is very cooling in summer. Levelled and polished, it creates a crisp and modern interior.

Between these two extremes lie natural fibres, lino and rubber, all of which have their particular pros and cons. Seagrass and hessian are strong textures and can sometimes overpower rooms containing modern furniture. They are also not particularly hard-wearing, so well-trodden circulation routes will wear before the rest. Lino tends to age relatively well as layers of wax and dirt slowly deepen the surface. Rubber, on the other hand, will require yearly cleaning and

ECOTIP

Planning for the future
One of the principles of ecoliving is to furnish your home with items that will stay with you for years. Constantly changing your décor to suit your furniture, or vice versa, is expensive on the pocket as well as the environment. Living-room furniture should be selected especially carefully because, if well chosen, it should adapt to your changing needs, and move with you from one home to the next. Never rush into selecting furniture and fittings, and be sure to refer to the ecological checklist in Chapter 7. In this way, you will ensure that your purchases really do stand up to the test of time.

v everyone's favourite

The sofa is probably the most expensive and long-lasting item of furniture in the living room, so choose carefully. As well as comfort, consider removable covers for easy cleaning and fire retardant material.

polishing if it is to maintain its as-new finish, so bear this in mind.

Rather than fitting wall-to-wall carpets, consider using mats and rugs that can be aired and dusted outside and replaced individually. Tiles and slates are best used more sparingly, either as bases to an old fireplace or as a centrepiece to a living space. An unpolished slab sitting at the centre of a warm living room appears strange, but it will provide an interesting base for a pile of magazines or a gnarled piece of wood or bark.

SHELVING SOLUTIONS

Living rooms are full of books, music, games and your favourite art, so you will need somewhere to store all of this. To retain an architectural rigour you might prefer fixed shelving with an even

light options

Small table lamps provide pools of light that wash walls or favourite reading areas (right). Large floor-to-ceiling windows allow lots of natural daylight into the room (below).

< low-level lounging
Sometimes relaxing on the floor is just as important as sitting on a comfortable chair, so furnish your living room with lots of rugs, cushions and beanbags.

spacing between the shelves. However, if your aim is to pack in as many books as possible, then adjustable shelving with pegged uprights and brackets is a must.

THE CEILING

The living room ceiling is as important as the floors and a poorly decorated ceiling will let the rest of the room down.

The usual plasterboard ceiling hides wiring and provides fire-protection between floors. In its simple way, it is a neat solution but it does make moving light fittings a hassle and it adds little to the character of the room. In old buildings it may be possible to expose the joists and bring a touch of age to an otherwise modern space. You may want to avoid the issue of ceiling lights altogether and use floor and table lamps instead. This will also leave a flat plane of colour above your head.

Choose a light colour to increase the feeling of space and only consider a dark ceiling finish if your ceiling is very high or you have large windows.

FIREPLACES

For many of us, the traditional fireplace remains the true focal point of the living room, with its mantelpiece housing our most

treasured possessions. While an open fire is inefficient and not particularly healthy, the common alternative of a blank wall and radiator is hardly inspirational.

Outside major cities, wood fires are still allowed, but they are banned from most urban settings to reduce city smog and pollution (use smokeless fuel instead). To reduce smoke levels in the countryside, use well-dried wood. You can also help to minimise environmental damage by burning fallen trees and wood thinnings.

To make a truly environmental fire, burn wood in a stove with a back-boiler and wrap the flue and pipes in a thick brick or concrete wall so that the heat can be stored in the living room but spread through the rest of your home.

CLOSE-UP: THE DAYBED

While sofas make comfortable places for lounging, they are often one-track items of furniture that don't offer much flexibility. Also, they are usually constructed from a complex mix of foam, metal springs and cheap wood by-products that are hard to fix or recycle. An interesting alternative is the modern chaise longue, the daybed. This should consist of a solid wooden frame made from beech or oak. To complement its one arm rest, it should also have lots of comfortable feather cushions.

Kitchens and cooking

Today's kitchen is no longer a utility but a festival, filled with different textures, colours and smells. It is your home's soul and hearth, and provides you with food, warmth and comfort. Rather than hiding this vital room away, make the kitchen a significant space in your home.

ALLOCATION

If the layout of your home allows it, consider having a combined kitchen and diner. In smaller homes, ignore the formality of two separate cooking and dining rooms and open up a galley kitchen to the living room instead.

If you are building your kitchen from scratch and have a choice, situate it beside the garden or balcony so that you have easy access to light. Do not make the kitchen the sole occupant of the outside wall, however, as living rooms also need light and views.

Organise the layout of the kitchen so that you can flow smoothly from storage to preparation to cooking with adequate space for each. By putting the sink and cooker on the same surface, there will be less chance of spilling hot water when moving pots and pans about. Make sure you give yourself enough work surface either side of the sink and the hob, and allow plenty of room for waste separation and disposal around the preparation zone.

Ideally, there should be just a few paces between the preparation area, oven and sink. Known as the kitchen triangle, this set-up allows you to work quickly, easily and safely.

UNFITTED KITCHENS

These are now becoming very popular and for good ecological reasons. First of all, they are made from more durable materials than the melamine-faced chipboard characterising fitted kitchens. Secondly, they can be moved around a room or taken with you

> room with a view

When planning your kitchen space, utilise natural daylight by situating work surfaces next to windows. This way, you won't be working in your own shadow and will always have a good view.

> clean and tidy

If you prefer a more minimal look for your kitchen, consider flush-fitted cupboards. These allow you to keep your kitchen jumble out of sight and also cut down on maintenance. Foodstuff also stores better if kept cool and in the dark.

---

keywords > efficient   hygienic   organised   safe

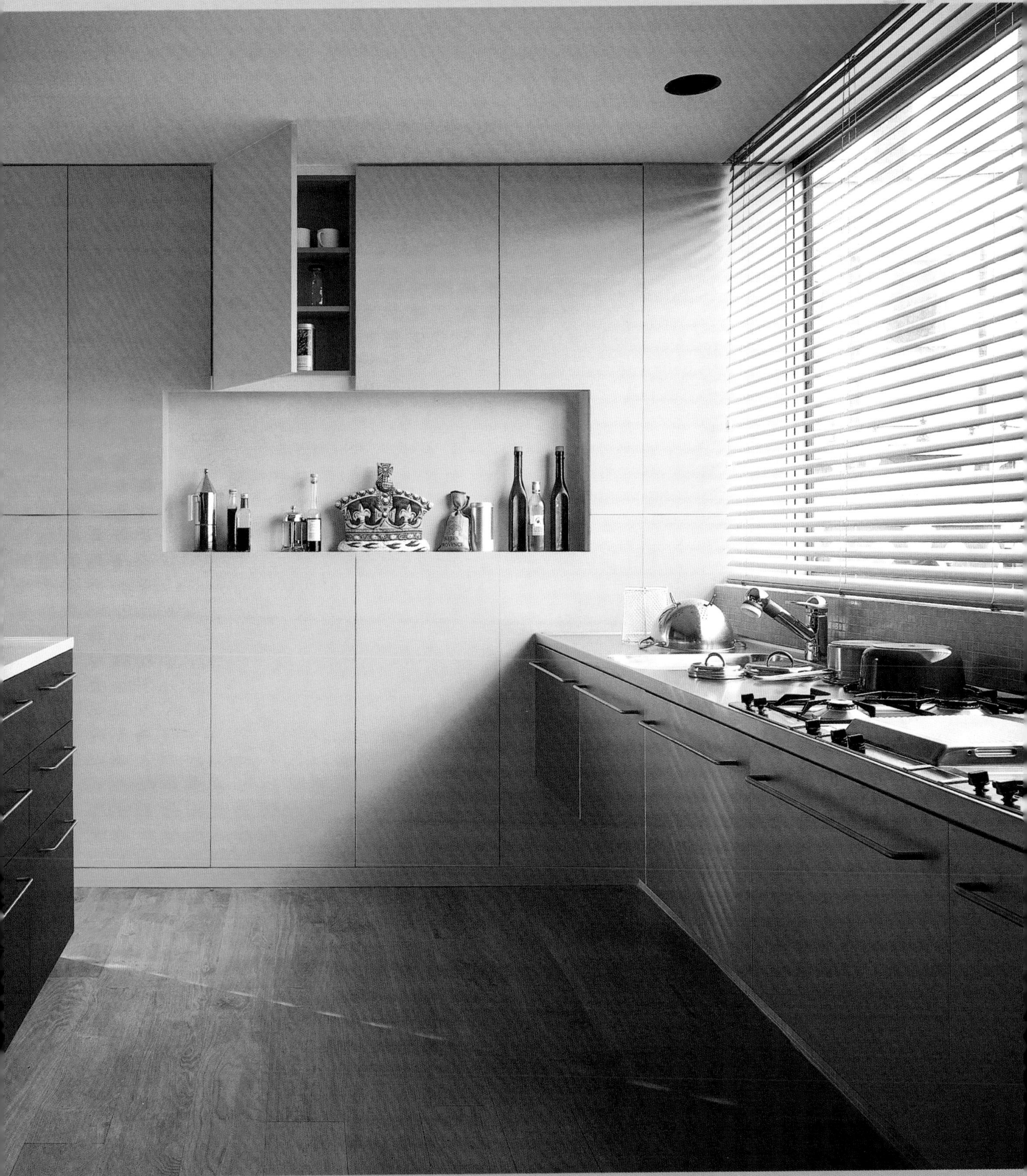

The Shaker kitchen

This group of devout Christians formed towards the end of the 18th century in England before moving to the United States. Apart from their combined skills in agriculture and forestry, the Shakers became renowned for their high quality furniture that was simple, practical and durable. Shaker furniture is traditionally made from local woods such as American oak and hickory, but there is no reason why these ideals can't be brought to life using woods that are found closer to home. To copy the Shaker style in your kitchen, think minimal. Keep only a few items of well-made furniture and decorate in plain or subdued colours. One popular Shaker habit is to hang chairs on hooks on the walls when they are not being used. This creates more space in the kitchen and also makes the floor easier to clean.

if you move home. Finally, the combination of solid wood, removable stone, stainless steel or timber worktops allows you to mix and match modern appliances with the older ones.

STORAGE IDEAS

Bearing in mind that fresh food should be stored in cool, well ventilated spaces shaded from the sun, make kitchen storage as pleasant as possible.

Avoid glass cabinets and containers (because food should be stored out of direct light) but remember that a row of colourful jars on a window shelf can be just as important for your well being as a well-ordered cupboard. Plan your shelving so that everything is

v hang and stack

Space is at a premium in a kitchen so take full advantage of every storage opportunity. Everyday items can hang on hooks attached to nearby walls and surfaces (below). Carousel shelves are good for less commonly used items (middle), while ceramic jars are good for storing basic ingredients (far right).

LIVING NATURALLY

Eating good food

Relearn the delights of food by practising the following habits:

• Choose local and fresh produce that is grown naturally and seasonally, stored carefully and prepared simply.

• Keep frozen and processed foods to a minimum and opt for more traditional storage methods, such as curing and preserving, as these keep foods fresh without the need for energy-consuming freezers.

• When buying foreign produce, stick to dry goods which are shipped at relatively little cost compared to the fresh stuff that requires air-freighting in cool boxes and leaves local farmers with less than a tenth of the consumer price.

• Avoid over-packaged goods, sticking to simple and easily recycled containers, such as bottles and paper, instead.

visible and within easy reach; make sure deeper pullout shelving is at a low level, while narrow adjustable shelves are high up.

SURFACES

Cooking is a messy business, so worktops, floors and walls should all be resistant to water, oil and kitchen smells. Terrazzo, polished concrete, ceramic, slate and stone are good choices for flooring as they are unaffected by heat or food and are very easy to keep clean. If you are prone to dropping

> ### splash-back tiles
Ceramic tiles are perfect materials for use in the kitchen because they are waterproof, easy to clean and ecofriendly, as well as economical.

things, then softer cork, linoleum or rubber floors will help to limit damage. Wood is another possibility although it is less resistant to water damage in the long run. A thick parquet floor with good joints is far better than thin timber veneers.

You need to be able to wipe these surface areas so avoid any delicate paintwork. Ceramic tiles add scale, colour and individuality, while stainless steel sheeting creates a cool modern finish that is long-lasting, easy to clean with mild detergents and adds the illusion of space to smaller rooms. Stainless steel can also be recycled at the end of its useful life. On other walls, try using tough mineral paint, cork or timber panelling.

WASTE

The kitchen should be the front-line for controlling waste disposal, especially since so much of it is generated there. Keep a bin for compostable food and make sure you have enough space inside for

< ### working surfaces
There are plenty of work surfaces to choose from and you should aim for quality over cost. Granite is a good choice because, although it is expensive, it is impervious to all it encounters. To avoid backache, make sure your benchtops are built to a suitable height.

the separation of items that you can either reuse in the home, take to the recycle centre, or dispose of completely. The basic categories that you need to allow for are compostable foodstuffs, paper and fabric, metals, glass, plastic, toxins and mixed waste. If you watch what goes into the waste bin and aim to avoid buying produce with unnecessary packaging, you can reduce waste by at least a half. For more information on ecofriendly waste disposal, see Chapter 6.

GETTING THE LIGHT RIGHT
It is vital that the kitchen is lit in such a way that you can prepare

∧ light and clean
Maximise daylight by leaving windows unobscured, placing a table by the window and keeping kitchen surfaces light in colour. This light, limestone kitchen floor is not only ecofriendly, it also creates a stunning, yet simple ambience.

ECOTIP

Low-energy cooking
The best eco-cooking methods are either to heat ingredients quickly on a high heat or to slowly stew them at a low temperature. Pressure cookers, microwave ovens, steamers and quick stir-frying all use a lot less energy than baking or boiling in open pans. When you do use the oven, get the most out of the heat by cooking in bulk. Better still, avoid using energy in the first place by making lots of salads and eating seasonal fruits.

food hygienically and safely. Maximise daylight by having a table next to the window and making sure that the window is unobscured by furniture or tall plants. Decorating kitchen surfaces in a pale colour will further help to reflect daylight.

As for electric lighting, small linear fluorescent tubes are an excellent and efficient source of lighting for food preparation and cooking areas. You can also use them inside glass cabinets to show off your favourite china.

ENERGY SAVING MEASURES
Simple technological innovations, such as a level mark on your kettle or the timer on your oven, will go a long way in preventing you

Despite the homey qualities associated with Agas, these cookers are relatively expensive to run, so are really only suitable for very large families who have a continuous demand for hot food and water. Urban dwellers should stick to gas cookers which use less fuel than electric ones and switch on and off at the touch of a button. They should also be cool to touch, so choose ovens with good wall insulation.

Ventilation

Because gas hobs produce fumes and cooking food produces steam and odours, it's important to install an extract system in the kitchen which draws out air when you are cooking. Recirculating cooker extract hoods do not solve the problem and only remove some of the grease and steam.

Ideally you should install an extractor hood connected to a heat exchange unit, so that the heat from cooking can be captured and returned to the house while moist air is channelled outdoors (see also page 40, Chapter 2). If this is not possible, then make sure the extract fan only runs when it is absolutely needed.

∧ effective lighting
Low voltage downlights illuminate kitchen work surfaces and benchtops. They need to be carefully sited to avoid creating shadows when you work. Installing a dimmer switch will allow you to change the atmosphere from a practical working space to a more intimate eating area.

from using energy in a wasteful manner, so try to fit out your kitchen with these items. Avoid filling the kettle with more water than you need, and try not to rely too much on electrical gadgets such as whisks when manual ones work just as well. Purchasing a pressure cooker or microwave oven will also reduce the amount of energy you use to cook.

The optimum cooker
If you live in a rural area, wood burning stoves will provide a renewable source of power both for cooking and for heating. The classic kitchen stove is being continually updated with modern versions able to run cleanly with low wood consumption, using back boilers to supply hot water and heat the home.

> economy measures
When choosing kitchen equipment for your ecofriendly home, always consider energy efficiency over style. Take advantage of technological advances by buying a combined fridge/freezer (top), a cooker with an air cleansing hood (middle) and a microwave oven (bottom).

An alternative low energy system is to use passive stack vents to draw the warm air from the room naturally, but this can only be used if you have direct access to the roof.

The fridge-freezer
A high-efficiency combination fridge-freezer will use relatively little power but still have room for all your basic needs. To keep it running at its best, defrost it every 6 months and keep it well stacked. Try not to freeze too much food, keep your fridge/freezer as compact as possible and never put warm items in the fridge.

CLOSE-UP: POTS AND PANS

You should only ever need to buy one set of pots and pans, so carefully consider the materials they are made from and the craftsmanship involved in making them. Stainless steel is a hard wearing material but pots need to have an aluminium or copper base for good heat conduction and retention. Aluminium pans share the same qualities as stainless steel, but some say they affect the taste of certain foods. All pots and pans should have straight sides that are fairly deep. Their lids should fit snugly and the handle should be sturdy, welded to the pan and have a hole from which to hang when storing. Classic enamelled cast-iron pots can last a century and are always worth the investment.

Dining rooms and eating

As a family, sitting down together for an evening meal and catching up on the day's events should be one of the most important times of the day. A separate dining area not too far away from the kitchen is the ideal place for this. With some fancy place settings and additional décor, this room can take on a more formal air and be used to entertain friends and colleagues.

MULTIFUNCTIONAL

The traditional dining table sits in its own room surrounded by space for ten chairs waiting for a purpose in life. This can be a waste of space and precious resources, so aim to use your dining room more often, perhaps as a place of study or where your kids can do their homework. Better yet, choose folding, sliding and dismountable surfaces. Tables in their simple form are legs and tops, and if you buy separates you will be able to take off the table top and lean it against the wall, creating extra floor space on which children can play or guests can stay over.

THE DINING TABLE

In addition to comfort, surface and shape should be your primary considerations when choosing a dining table. Those that are round and oval will make conversation easier and have no sharp or

< dress up or down
A cheap and easy way to change the atmosphere of your dining room to suit the occasion is with fabric chair coverings and table-cloths.

∧ dual purpose

If space is at a premium in your home, use your dining room as a study area. A large dining table is also an ideal place for kids to sit down and do their homework together.

< close to the source

A partition with backlighting creates the illusion of a separate dining area, while still having the convenience of being close to the kitchen.

awkward corners. However, square and rectangular-shaped tables are easier to move against the wall when you want to use the room for another purpose. Consider a table with fold-out flaps for ultimate adaptability. Hard materials, such as marble, glass and slate are easy to maintain, although wood is the most relaxing surface. As for table linen, choose fabric cloths and napkins to soften non-wooden surfaces and use hard mats and paper napkins to create the opposite effect.

Suitable materials

When choosing a dining table, remember that it will be used frequently and, no matter how careful you are, will still suffer from food spillages and damage

v wood, glorious wood

Sustainable timber in all its forms is light, long lasting and easy to clean so it is the ideal material for dining furniture. Chairs should be comfortable, so if they don't have upholstery, attach a cushion to their seats.

two of a kind
Nothing beats fine bone china as the ultimate, long-lasting, classically attractive material for crockery (above right). However, you might like to purchase some cheap and cheerful items for everyday use (above left).

guarded to protect them against stains. Solid wood or metal chairs may be a better choice when you have young children, but whatever material you choose, they should all give firm support for the back and spine.

FLOORING

The best flooring materials for the dining room are those that are hardwearing and easy to sweep or wipe clean. Stripped or polished floorboards and linoleum or cork tiles are all good choices. Because food gets dropped, drinks get spilled and candles leak melted wax, carpet is not a good idea. If wall-to-wall carpeting is already in place, position your table on top of a rug. If you have children, consider putting a sheet of plastic under the table to catch all the crumbs and keep your floor clean.

from sharp or hot implements. Wood is the ideal choice for a dining table. Veneer coated tables will damage quickly so protect them by placing a felt underlay and tablecloth on top. Solid oak, beech and even softwoods like pine are excellent woods for tables, provided they are protected with hard wax oils.

While cheaper melamine and plywood is less attractive, you can always cover it with a favourite table-cloth, which hides the less than perfect top and allows kids to scribble on it during the day.

DINING CHAIRS

Chairs should complement both the table and the room itself. Stacking chairs are good because they are space saving and can be used to add interest to the walls if hung up. Director's chairs are

multi-purpose and you can usually buy alternative seats and backs. This not only prolongs their useable life, but is also an easy way to change your décor. Upholstered chairs in natural fibres are now commonplace and are the most comfortable form of seating. Coverings can even be scotch-

< cloth versus paper
Good quality linen napkins will last a lifetime and are much more ecofriendly than disposable ones. Wrapping them in silver napkins holders will also bring a touch of class to the table.

Bedrooms and sleeping

This is the simplest room to decorate because it really only has a few purposes: to help you sleep, dream, make love and wake up refreshed. A generous and comfortable bed is the key to achieving these but, unfortunately, we seem to fill the bedroom with other distractions that merely add to the clutter in our lives. Making the bedroom a store, a dressing room, the make-up parlour or an alternative study can all lead to complicated solutions.

LOCATION AND LAYOUT

Bedrooms demand privacy, peace and a little natural light. Ideally, choose a room that catches the early morning sun, away from noise and pollution. Since it is very much a night time room, alternative locations towards the north of your home will also work, whereas south-facing bedrooms waste valuable sunshine that would better benefit daytime activities. In warm climates, the bedroom should definitely be kept shady and cool, with good access to natural breezes.

For privacy, separate the children's rooms from the parents', perhaps using the bathroom as an intermediate room. The French architect Corbusier went one step further and, in his Unite d'Habitation, placed the parents' bedrooms at one end of the flat, close to the living room with the kids' bedroom at the opposite end.

Bedrooms may seem strange on the ground floor of your home but don't be afraid of considering this more radical approach. If the windows are sheltered from direct view, they may actually be more suited on this floor because it is generally cooler at night and there is more privacy.

THE BED

In the East, the bed is often little more than a thickening of the floor matting and a traditional futon laid directly on the bedroom floor is a neat and simple solution for a restful night. During the day it can be rolled up and away or taken outside to air when needed.

The downside of a futon is that it doesn't give you a comfortable

differing needs

The bed you choose for your children will obviously be different from your own, but both should be easy to dismantle for portability and optimum flexibility.

choice for an evening read or breakfast in bed and that's where the western bed-head and base come into their own. Beds that don't lie low to the ground also have the benefit of providing storage space out of view.

Bed bases

These come in many shapes and sizes, the standard being the fabric covered box base, which is neither attractive nor long lasting. The better alternative is to buy simple slatted wood bases that you can varnish with linseed-based oils to match your décor.

Mattresses

While futons are made from simple cotton wadding, western mattresses are constructed from metal springs and synthetic foams. Obviously, the more you pay the more you will get in return and an expensive mattress lasts longer and provides more support for your back. That said, a firm futon that is properly cared for offers all the support that you need.

SUITABLE SURFACES

The bedroom floor is perhaps the one place in your home where a more luxurious floor finish will

∧ occasional beds

Futons are ideal for storing away until you have a guest. Not only do futons take up far less space than western mattresses, but they can also be used as a sofa when placed on a fold-up base.

add to your comfort and be relatively easy to maintain.

A timber block floor will provide a clean surface and the addition of a thick rug at the base of your bed or to its side will give your feet a comfortable and warm landing. In comparison, a stone floor might simply shock you into action. If you have a no-shoes policy, then you may want to use a fitted wool carpet, although the fact that most of it will sit under the bed or other furniture does makes its use debatable. Alternatively, you may prefer the rough texture of natural fibres, such as coir matting. The key is choosing a floor that is easy to keep dust-free. This way, the air in your bedroom encourages ease and rest, rather than antagonising your lungs.

LIGHTING

In the bedroom, lighting should be relatively subdued and close to hand. Bedside and table lamps are far better options than overhead fittings. Directional task lamps can either point towards the wall for a gentle wash of light or provide excellent directed light for late night reading without disturbing your sleeping partner. Lighting is also useful at the dressing table and by wardrobes.

keep it neat
Ideal bedroom storage should be fitted, making it a part of the room's repertoire. Cleverly concealed cupboards made from ash wood can even double up as an extended headboard (right). If you choose free-standing pieces of furniture, make sure they are made from natural, ecofriendly materials (above).

Eternally yours: the bed-head

In the past, the ornately carved marital bed-head was a fitting part of the new family's dowry and was treasured from youth to old age before being handed down to the next generation. If the idea of sleeping in your parents' or grandparents' bed is a little disconcerting, seek out an old-fashioned bed frame or bed-head in your local antique store.

If you are a heavy sleeper, choose some lightweight curtains that will allow the morning light to filter through. Light sleepers will require thicker, lined curtains to ensure lie-ins on the weekends.

DECORATION IDEAS

Many bedrooms today have either a virginal or sensual air. Some people prefer the rich tapestry of

exotic art, while others treat the bedroom as a clean, almost monastic, cell.

Although there are fewer ecological considerations in the bedroom than the other rooms of your home, the following thoughts will give you an idea of how you might go about decorating.

The sensuous bedroom will have rich and deep colours that create an enclosure around your bed, with subdued lighting. Conversely,

a white bedroom with pale wood and light fabrics will need little artificial lighting during the day and will help you to rise with the sun. However, it may seem too clinical at night, particularly when the moon shining through curtains casts an eerie light.

Decorating the ceiling

Perhaps our lasting memories of the childhood bedroom are small fluorescent stars twinkling in the

darkened ceiling of a sky as we slowly drifted off to slumber land.

While this imagery is overblown in adulthood, it does serve to remind us that the ceiling is an important design element in the bedroom. Where they might have disappeared in other rooms of your home, poor quality light fittings and badly finished wallpaper will remain an eyesore in the bedroom. While a simply painted ceiling might be all that's

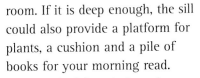

< the feminine touch
A crystal chandelier and a restored rococo mirror placed on a soft lilac background creates a feeling of understated opulence.

needed, consider alternative ceiling finishes, such as tongue and groove timber panelling, as these add character to your nightly view.

Window effects

The bedroom window itself may be the perfect space to start decorating your eco-bedroom.

A light-painted sill and surrounds make a perfect place to let the morning diffuse into the room. If it is deep enough, the sill could also provide a platform for plants, a cushion and a pile of books for your morning read.

The end of the window alcove provides a neat space for a set of thick curtains that will keep the heat in at night. Alternatively you might set a bed platform itself at sill height so that you can wake with an immediate view of the outside world, with cooling air at hand on a sultry summer night.

LINEN

This should be easy to clean and long lasting. Avoid synthetic sheets and blankets because they attract dust and don't allow your

∧ early morning call
Using an old-fashioned wind-up alarm clock is a way to avoid electromagnetic radiation and unnecessary use of electricity in the bedroom.

skin to breathe properly. Duck down duvets are a practical and easy care alternative, although feather fills are allergenic for some (see pages 82–83, Chapter 3).

Polyester duvet fillings are available at a lower cost and can last for an equally long time. Always store duvets that are made with feather fillings and natural fibre bed linen in warm and dry conditions so they are safe from moths and damp air.

Mattress pads are also advisable because not only will they keep the mattress cleaner for longer, they will also provide extra warmth and softness.

< fresh and fancy
Linen is the ideal fabric for bedding because not only is it a long-lasting ecofriendly material, but it is also cool against the skin in summer.

Bathrooms and bathing

Although a necessity, washing is the one time and place in the day where we can contemplate our navels in peace, away from the frenzy of modern living. In many homes, the bathroom is hidden away and filled with pastel fibreglass and plastics, vinyl flooring, bare and washed out tungsten bulbs and a whirring extract fan: practical possibly, but hardly natural, inspiring or long lasting. But times are changing and we are beginning to relearn the gentle art of bathing, taking the functional and hidden out of the closet and talking happily about hygiene, sewage and wash efficiencies.

and ventilation help to create a more relaxing environment. Also, modifications to plumbing are easier to make when there is access to an outside wall. If there is space under the stairs or at the end of a corridor, consider building a separate room for the toilet. Not only is this convenient, it creates more room for a bathing space and it is also healthier to separate the two very different basic needs.

Try to avoid having more than one bathroom per home as this uses more space, more material and generally leads to more use (or waste). If you do need more bathing space, create a shower room instead.

LOCATION

In most homes a bathroom's location is fixed by the existing plumbing. Unless you can clearly see a better way of arranging your home, you will most likely have to make the most of things with this limitation. If you can relocate, try moving the bathroom to an outer wall as the resulting natural light

BATHROOM FURNITURE

The furniture that we choose for our bathrooms lasts longer than in any other room in our home, so ensuring that they are both beautiful and efficient is vitally important. Collectively, the bath, toilet, shower and basin use three

> bathing in grandeur

If you have enough space in your bathroom, install a free-standing bath and take the art of bathing to a higher level. Free-standing baths also provide a focal point in large bathrooms.

> internal warmth

Surrounded by other centrally heated rooms in your home, the bathroom is usually quite easy to heat and keep warm. Heated towel rails also encourage warmth and if your bathroom doesn't have a window, view this positively because it will also help to keep heat in.

quarters of the entire water supply for your home and the energy used to heat water might make up half your total gas or electricity bills. It's especially important, therefore, to be mindful of water and energy conservation methods when choosing these items.

Decide whether free-standing or fitted equipment suits your bathroom best. A free-standing bath and shower provide a focal point to larger bathrooms, while a fitted bath tiled into the wall and floor will provide the best use of space in a smaller one.

BATHS AND SHOWERS

In Roman times, daily bathing was a public and shared experience, moving from the changing rooms through a hot scrub bath (the caldarium), to the bustling and noise-filled warm pool (the tepidarium) and a final plunge into the cold frigidarium. The public baths were a sign of civilisation and often one of the first buildings to be built after vanquishing a neighbouring barbarian town. Private baths were rare and even emperors used to make occasional visits to the public pools.

But Roman cleanliness was particular to the time and place. By the Middle Ages, bathing was

bathing space
In smaller bathrooms, a shower over the bath provides you with two bathing options (above). If you have more space available, then you can even consider installing a bidet for added hygiene (left).

< salvage solutions
Architectural reclamation yards are great sources of old baths. If you find a copper bath, make sure it's small because, being a conductor of heat, your water will cool quickly.

stepping out
A bamboo bath mat is water-resistant and more durable than other materials (top). If you prefer a softer landing, however, use a cotton bath mat (above).

considered dangerous because it was thought to upset the thermal equilibrium of our bodies. Instead, people used perfumes to hide body odour. It was only in the 18th century, when doctors began to recognise the importance of clean air and clean water, that a daily wash became fashionable again.

∧ **bathroom tidy**

If you like to have your bathing accessories at hand, choose a shower hanger with a durable and tarnish-resistant finish.

∧ **shower safety**

Shower trays come in several shapes and sizes, which means you can install a shower cubicle in almost any corner of your bathroom. Make sure the cubicle is well-fitted, with a well-sealed door that prevents water from splashing onto the floor outside. Specially sealed spotlights are also available for this benefit. Always cover shower walls with water-resistant tiles.

And it wasn't until the 19th century and the arrival of cholera from the East that the first municipally supplied fresh water and fast-flowing sewers allowed us the enjoyment of taking a bath every day. Even today, a daily tub of warm water is a luxury in most parts of the world.

Hygienically and ecologically, showers beat baths bottoms down. They flush away the day's dirt or the night's sleep more rapidly than a dip in a bath, using less water and less energy than a bath. Yet nothing compares to a good, long soak in the comfort and privacy of your own bathtub. Use your own

judgement to achieve a balance between comfort, hygiene and care for resources.

The ideal shower is one that uses minimal water but provides an invigorating wash. Avoid the modern power showers as these can use even more water than a conventional bath. Instead, opt for specially adapted shower heads that aerate the water, but restrict the total volume. Avoid electrically heated water systems as these use two to three times as much energy as gas-heated hot water supplies.

Plastic baths don't require a lot of energy for their manufacture, but they scratch easily and will look worn and old more quickly. If you can, look for smaller and deeper traditional cast iron baths. Many of these have been replaced by fibreglass or plastic tubs, which

classic colours
White sanitary ware (top) offers
the maximum flexibility, whereas
a coloured suite is likely to lose
its visual appeal over time and
therefore is more likely to be
replaced. Alternatively, opt for a
clean, modern metal look (above).

are fairly harmless ecologically,
but are neither as beautiful nor as
long-lasting as their cast iron or
pressed steel equivalents. If you
have an old cast iron bath with
scratches, instead of replacing it,
get it re-enamelled and save
yourself some money and the
scrap heap some waste.

Toilets

In the 18th century, way before
the flush toilet was invented,
defecation was a relatively public
affair and we used to chat away to
friends whilst perched on the
chaise-perce under which was
hidden the chamber pot. In the
19th century this gave way to the
privy. The toilet bowl transcended
mere utilitarian concerns and
became an object of private
comfort, fitted out with magazine
racks, cast with ornamental
designs and culminating in a
design by the eponymous Mr
Crapper. To this day, the world is
still divided between those who
use the toilet as a small-scale
private library and those who
want to get it all over with as
quickly and effectively as possible.

Many homes are still fitted with
older toilets that use up to12 litres
of water each flush. With little
effort, this can be reduced by a
quarter, simply by putting a couple
of bricks in the cistern (or the
patented inflatable 'Hippo'). Better
still, replace older loos with a dual
flush loo that allows you to decide
whether you need a 3 litre or a 6
litre flush. The toilet pans are
specially shaped so that they
remove waste efficiently with
minimum water.

At the most ecological end of
the market, it is possible to buy a
number of composting toilets.
These use no water and create
perfectly good compost for your
garden. Although they cost more
than the savings you'll make from
reduced water use, they do make

economic sense in low-water
regions and in situations when
you are aiming to be
completely self-sufficient.

Most commercial toilet paper
is made from bleached paper in
a high-energy process. Non-
bleached recycled papers may
be less luxurious, but they are
cheaper, often decompose more
quickly and are just as
effective. They are a must if
you are considering treating
sewage waste in the garden.

Basins

These are generally available in
porcelain or stainless steel,
both of which are long-lasting
and environmentally
responsible materials. See if
you can get them fitted with

∨ basin basics

Butler sinks are a popular choice in many
modern homes, but they require huge
quantities of water to fill. It is much
easier to wash your face in a shallow
basin, and you'll waste less water too.

∧ au naturel

Not only does a wet shave give a much better result than an electric shaver, it is also a much better eco-choice. This is because you don't need to install special shaver sockets in your bathroom and you don't use electricity. Always avoid plastic, disposable razors.

spray taps that reduce the amount of water you use by aerating the water through fine nozzles. The resulting spray is just as effective at wetting and cleaning your skin, but it halves the amount of water you use. Existing taps can be modified with simple (although it has to be said, not very attractive) adaptors, or you can buy well-designed new taps if you are upgrading your bathroom. Always use a plug rather than letting water straight out of the hole when washing your face or hands.

Keep your medicines and toiletries in a lockable cabinet above the sink. Open shelves are not a good idea for storing make-up and medicine because they gather dust easily. Ceramic or glass dishes are good for holding soap

and if you buy attractive or textured types they will be beautiful objects in themselves.

Spare towels and laundry can be kept in a louvered cupboard which will help to keep the bathroom tidy. If you have a hot water cylinder in your bathroom, consider building a cupboard around it – it is great for drying and airing clothes and towels you

have just washed. As for drying wet towels, a simple towel rail connected to the central heating will serve this purpose while keeping your bathroom warm at the same time. In the absence of a heated towel rail, keep the towels you are using on a clothes horse, which allows you to spread them out evenly to dry. Towels and robes don't tend dry very well on

CLOSE-UP: BATH SOAPS

Natural soaps and cleansing oils will help to create colour in the bathroom and are also more friendly, both for you and the environment. There are now a wide range of soaps made with vegetable bases such as palm, coconut oil and jojoba oils. Translucent glycerine soaps are less alkaline than ordinary soaps and also give an attractive effect. Milk and honey soaps are good for sensitive skins. Other effective bath additives include epsom salts, which help to relax muscles and joints; aromatherapy oils; and herbs. Similarly, oatmeal or bran can be tied in a square of muslin, hung from the hot tap and hot water allowed to run through. Both grains have a soothing effect on the skin.

a peg on the back of the door, and could also contribute to creating a somewhat musty, mouldy atmosphere in the bathroom.

Cleaning fluids should be kept separately from toiletries so store these and other less attractive bathroom necessities in low-level cupboards under the sink or under raised decks next to the bath and shower area.

BATHROOM SURFACES

If they are to last a long time and remain beautiful, bathroom floors and walls need to be watertight, slip resistant and able to cope with heat and moisture.

Good flooring options for the bathroom include cork, linoleum, terrazzo or local slate. Avoid carpets, natural fibre or wood because these are all prone to water damage, harbour mould and require frequent replacement.

Ceramic tiles provide a beautiful, reliable and long-lasting finish, and can handle any volume of water without damage. They can also be thoroughly washed to help maintain a clean and healthy environment. If tiling a whole wall proves too expensive, confine it to splash-backs around the bath and sink, and use external-quality plaster, either bare or with a tint of natural colour added to the mix, for the rest of the wall.

WINDOWS

Where possible, a bathroom should have a window to allow in natural light and which you can open to aid ventilation. The sunlight can

∧ take your pick

There is a huge array of materials with which to decorate your bathroom walls and floors. Depending on the colours, textures and patterns you choose, these can help you transform a functional utility space into a stylish and relaxing room. Suitable bathroom materials include (clockwise from top left) rubber tiles, special paints for revitalising old vinyl floor tiles, ceramic tiles and stone tiles.

be diffused through a linen blind for privacy or through forest friendly plants and shrubs placed on the window sill for a tropical feel. If your window has a private view, let the stars shine in at night. In cooler climates, use low e double-glazing (see page 38, Chapter 2) as this reduces both heat loss and condensation that forms on cold surfaces.

Protect wooden window frames and sills from warping with water-resistant wax or water-resistant natural paints. Tiled sills and surroundings are easier to maintain because they are more water resistant, and light coloured tiles are even better because they reflect daylight into the room. Slotted brickwork (bricks laid with holes between) or timber louvres

are good window options because not only do they allow adequate levels of ventilation and light to filter through, they also connect your bathroom to the outdoors. If you do choose this option use wire-mesh to keep insects and other trouble makers on the right side of the window.

LIGHTING

While natural light can provide just the bathroom atmosphere you want, you'll need to consider night-time lighting too. Perhaps the lowest energy lighting is candle light. Other low-energy lights for bathrooms include compact flourescent bulbs, mini

lighting and atmosphere

Combined with your favourite incense, candle light provides a soothing background glow while you bathe (left). If you can, arrange your bathroom in a room facing the rising sun (below). This way, you will be able to soak up the early morning sunshine as you luxuriate in the water.

flourescent tubes and halogen spot lights (see pages 25–28, Chapter 2). Lighting levels can be low throughout the bathroom, but with a more intense light source near the bathroom mirror for make-up, shaving and checking out the medicine cabinet.

VENTILATION

It is especially important that the bathroom is well ventilated since moist air and surfaces easily become traps for bacteria and mould. Ventilation is also paramount in keeping this room fresh and clean. An electrically operated extract fan, the natural chimney effect of a passive stack vent or simply an open window are the best ways to achieve good ventilation.

Extract fans

Although these run on electricity, only a small amount of energy is consumed in return for a good level of ventilation. By connecting extract fans to a light switch or using a humidity controller, the fan will run only when it is really needed, limiting its energy use even further. The first rule for installing an extract fan in the bathroom is to make sure it is a quiet one, since nothing is more inhibiting to relaxation than the incessant drone of a noisy fan. The second consideration is to ensure that it is neither too big nor too small for the job.

You can also buy bathroom fans with balanced air heat exchangers, which recover the energy in the exhaust air (see page 40, Chapter 2). These units are provided with two fans, one to push air into the room and one to draw air out. The cold outside air is drawn through a series of metal plates that are warmed by the exhaust air and recover about 60 per cent of the heat. They are good energy savers in cold climates, but not really necessary if you keep the bathroom cool.

Passive stack vents

These act like miniature chimneys in your bathroom and should also be fitted with light and humidity controllers to avoid throwing away warm house air. The chimney is made from a small plastic pipe with a vent outlet in the roof.

When the passive stack vent is open, any wind passing over the roof helps to draw warm air out of the bathroom. These vents can be used only if your bathroom has easy access to a roof, and are most successful when installed at the top of a pitched roof.

< made to last

The thick pile that constitutes traditional bath towels also makes them prone to mildew and bacteria because they are hard to dry. The alternative waffle towel is ultra absorbent, but also quick-drying.

Studies and home working

Working from home can be the best or the worst of both worlds. For some, it means packing in the daily commute to the big smoke and being able to spend more time with the family. For others, it can seem like a jail sentence, stuck between the same four walls, unable to share ideas, meet new people or discover the rest of the world.

Successful home-working usually happens when you make a conscious effort to separate work from the other aspects of your home life. There is nothing worse than waking up to see a computer terminal staring unblinking from the dressing table or to find paints and other art materials scattered around the kitchen. If you work from home, it is a good idea to have some sort of transitional process, be it mental or physical, to make the distinction between relaxing in your home and working in your home. A gentle stroll to the type-writer in the shed at the bottom of the garden or climbing up the last flight of stairs to the attic are

> classic bureaux

If you don't need a lot of work surface, consider a well-made wooden bureau. You might even be able to use the wooden desk you had as a child, which will give your office a more homey feel.

some examples of this. You should also hang a sign on your door, which indicates that you are working and are not to be disturbed.

SPACE REQUIREMENTS

These will naturally depend on what it is you do, but the general rule of thumb is that you'll need between 8 and 10m^2 of space. It is unlikely that you can give up so much of your home to this one activity, but where possible, try to make your office in a room that is separate from your general home life; a study or the spare room is ideal. The space needs to have good natural light and ventilation, which means having a window surface that is between 20 and 40 per cent of the floor area. Any less than this and the room will need artificial light for longer; any greater and it will overheat in the summer and require more heating in the winter.

SUITABLE DIRECTIONS

Art, writing and computer work are often best done in a north-facing room where the even light is kinder to the eyes. That said, a south-facing room is also fine if it has good adjustable external shading; an east-facing room will have gentle light in the afternoon when the sun has moved away.

unusual corners

If you don't have the luxury of dedicating a whole room to your study, you can still create office space with some careful planning. For rooms with high ceilings, an effective solution is to build a mezzanine, which will double the wall and floor space available to you and bring you closer to the light (left). Alternatively, convert the space under stairs (below).

Avoid rooms that are affected by the noise and pollution of passing traffic. A room with a pleasant view is preferable to one without.

Remember that work is far less stressful when everything has a place, so give yourself plenty of

ECOTIP

Efficient home working
Use a portable computer that consumes little space or energy, produces far less screen radiation and is easier to move around than a bulky desk-top machine. If you use a desk-top computer, make sure it's Energy Star compatible. Avoid using screen savers because, despite the name, they actually waste energy since the monitor is still on. Always aim to have multi-purpose equipment rather than lots of small items. Today, a single piece of equipment can act as a fax, telephone, printer and photocopier, and will use less space, energy and materials than the individual items combined. It often costs less as well. Email will reduce the amount of paper you use, which should always be recycled. When you print, use both sides, and reuse single-sided paper. When you do visit clients or colleagues, use your bike or public transport instead of the car.

> **office accessories**
A good desk lamp (right) is essential if you want to prevent eyestrain. Choose one that pivots for maximum flexibility. A diary bound in natural leather (centre) makes a classier alternative to electronic organisers, and a good fountain pen (bottom) is not only a joy to use, but also more ecological than disposable biros.

horizontal room both for laying out work and stacking work materials. When it comes to choosing desk accessories and storage systems, avoid the clinical look of most plastic or metal items and choose simple wooden ply boxes and holders that are gentler on the eye and the planet. Recycled cardboard magazine holders are fine for organising information and open wooden shelving on adjustable brackets will help you to store your files and accounts.

YOUR DESK AND LIGHTING
Obviously, the size of the desk you require will depend on the type of work you do, but it should always be long lasting and attractive.

The best position for your desk is next to an outside wall and at right angles to the window. This way, your eyes don't suffer from glare when you look up from your work. This will also make it far easier to open the window or close the blinds when the weather changes. Use a task lamp directly over your work area so that you can see clearly on overcast days.

Angle-poise lamps that have fluorescent or low-voltage halogen bulbs provide the most flexibility.

COMFORT AND QUALITY
Whatever work you do and however you do it, always make sure that you are working comfortably. If your work involves using a computer, make sure the monitor is at eye-level to reduce neck-strain. If you are doing manual work, set the bench height so that you don't have to bend over. Have an alternative place to work that allows you to stand and work at the same time, such as a high, tilted lectern with a flat, adjacent surface. Choose a chair that is adjustable and supports your lower back.

The overall atmosphere of your work environment is also important. Surround yourself with fond memories that will cheer you up through duller days, such as pictures of your family and friends or simple objects of nature. Fill the room with plants and water them when you're lost for words. As soon as cabin-fever strikes, get away from your desk.

Just as in the rest of your home, avoid toxic materials and energy-consuming appliances. Buy a nice, textured rug to add some colour to the room. Take your shoes off and stretch your toes: make the most of being your own office manager.

∨ easy-access files
Home-working tends to generate a lot of paperwork, so you will need plenty of shelving to store invoices and records of accounts. Choose files made from recycled cardboard and try to reuse them whenever possible.

Studios
and bedsits

As we become richer, there is an incessant desire to own bigger and better things. Living small demands an alternative vision. Size does matter, but sometimes the smaller something is, the better it can be. The key is to look for quality over quantity, things that last rather than things that shout.

GOOD PLANNING

One of the benefits of living small is that it is far easier to make the space your own, but you do need to be well organised so there is space for work, entertaining, sleep and relaxation. In nature, different plants and animals use the same space at different times of the day, and this 'stacking' is the key to making a success of small spaces.

Ceiling height

If you have the option, an extra half metre of ceiling height is more valuable than a few extra square metres of floor space. A taller, small room will not only

> compact and bijou
In a small kitchen, maximising the amount of work surface is particularly important. This can be achieved by mounting microwaves and other kitchen appliances onto the wall.

seem larger, it will also be brighter and capable of accommodating raised platforms, which add to the illusion of space. You can even locate the kitchen and shower room under a raised bed and storage platform or create level changes that provide additional storage space underneath them. A metre-wide platform half a metre above the floor will give you the feeling of entering a different space and also provide you with loads of low-level storage.

Clever plumbing

To minimise the space taken up by plumbing, make sure you locate your utility areas next to each other so that you can share items rather than duplicating them. One large sink might well be enough for washing both your face, your dishes and your clothes.

Illusions of grandeur

Light-coloured walls and floors create an illusion of space and spread daylight deeper into your home, which means you can use lower-wattage bulbs without straining your eyes. Having lots of windows and greenery will also increase the sense of space in a small home. Ideally, windows should reach down to the floor and floor surfaces inside and out

should merge with plants on either side of the glazing.

APPROPRIATE FURNITURE

Choose small furniture that is modular, mobile, fold-up or roll-away. Low-lying furniture, such as futons and coffee tables, are also preferable to high-backed chairs and tables as they will keep your visual horizon clear and help to maintain a spacious feeling.

Modular furniture multiplies your choices. Three small tables can either act separately as a sideboard, worktop and bedside dressing table, or they can be joined together to make a large dining table. Fold up a table so that it lies flat against a wall or stack chairs and hang them from a hook on the wall. Roll away a futon at the beginning of the day to convert a sleeping space into a work room. Use open, movable shelving that reaches from floor to ceiling to maximise the space you need for books and mementoes.

Finally, if all else fails, use mirrors to artificially expand your space. But take note of some old words of wisdom: moderation is far better than excess.

< one-room living

High ceilings that allow for 'stacking' or platform space are the key to having all your living areas in just one large room. Try to keep your home as clutter-free as possible because this will help to prevent you from feeling overcrowded by your possessions.

Basement living

O ften poorly decorated and under-performing, basements suffer from a lack of light, a propensity to leak water and are often cold year round. Even so, with a little imagination and careful improvement they can be converted into comfortable and low-energy additional living spaces.

WARM AND LIGHT

The first step to successful basement living is to remove damp and cold spots with appropriate water-proofing and insulation. Strip out old carpets as these might be concealing damp and holding in dust and mould. Repair damp patches and insulate old windows with draught-proofing tape and thick curtains. The next step is selecting a colour scheme that is both warming and light. Warmer wall finishes are suitable, particularly in living spaces where a plain white finish might not attract enough natural daylight to feel really welcoming.

Basement spaces usually have concrete floors, which make them very cold in winter. To achieve a warmer effect, both visually and physically, use a softer floor covering, such as linoleum. Alternatively you can seal the concrete with a rubber finish (adding comfort and colour with rugs), or lay an inch of insulation on the floor and cover this with a light timber board which will retain the warmth from your heating system, preventing its loss to the ground underneath.

Finally, try to pay as much attention to the outside perimeter of your basement space as you do to the inside. Render courtyards in a light mineral plaster or decorate the area with bright ceramic tiles. Link these outside spaces into your flat with the use of plants or common materials (use the same ceramic tiles inside and out, for example) as these will give the illusion of expanding the edges of your home.

> making an entrance
This lower ground space benefits from light coloured walls, large windows and an arched roof with exposed beams, giving the illusion of greater height.

> dining downstairs
If the structure of your home allows, consider knocking through the rooms in your basement to maximise the amount of light circulating. Open up the external walls as much as possible, too, to enhance your connection with the world just outside your windows.

Attics

In a crowded metropolis, one of the best places to live is on the top floor. Here you will receive more light, breathe cleaner air and have better, sometimes even panoramic, views.

Not all of us have the option to live in a high rise building, however, let alone its top floor. If this is your case, don't despair! You can still get the benefits of a warm, light-filled and resource-efficient space by carefully thinking through your options in order to convert your attic.

PLANNING

Loft living will work best if there is a south or west-facing aspect. If this isn't possible, then plan to convert the roof so that it has a sun-facing window with a low base which can be opened in summer. This way the whole of the attic room becomes an extension of the outdoors.

Use the gable ends or create flat-roofed loft extensions so that standard vertical windows can be installed. A number of smaller windows on two or three aspects will create views all around and enable you to receive even and varied natural light wherever you are in your home. Avoid installing windows in the pitch of the roof as these are prone to leaks, give poor views of the horizon and, if they face sunward, cause overheating in summer while letting in little solar warmth in winter.

v peaceful productivity

A study in the loft has the unique benefits of being warm, private and peaceful. This space can get hot at midday, but blinds will help to reduce the temperature, as well as any glare.

> the high life

If storage is a problem in your home, converting the loft will provide a good, practical solution. Shelving units will fit snugly under eaves and wall partitions can double up as extra wardrobe space.

Conservatories

This room is the ideal place between indoors and outdoors, between nature and our modern world. In summer, its open doors and windows allow the garden to seep through into the house, while in the winter the conservatory acts as an extra blanket against the winter cold.

The main benefit of conservatories is that they provide cheap and additional living space in the warmer months of the year. In addition, they can act as draught lobbies and, surrounded by growing plants and simple natural materials, make the perfect spot to spend time relaxing first thing in the morning or last thing at night. A solar conservatory will also act as a simple heat store.

SUITABLE LOCATIONS

The best direction for a solar conservatory is south-facing. However, an east or west-facing room will also collect warmth and provide extra

> additional rooms

Building a conservatory onto your home will not only have the benefit of letting in natural light, it may also create much needed space for a summer dining room.

insulation to your home. A west-facing room stays warm well into the evening, while an east-facing room provides warmth until mid-afternoon. Avoid a shady outlook that blocks the sun's heat and make sure your conservatory is constructed with a solid insulated floor and an air-tight timber and glass structure above.

In cold climates, the conservatory roof and walls should be double-glazed to prevent frost. In warm climates, the entire structure can be single-glazed, with a solid west wall and external roof shading to prevent the space from over-heating in summer.

Never heat a conservatory artificially and always separate it from your living room by double glazed windows and doors. Otherwise it will only add to your home's energy costs. This may seem like an imposition, particularly on a winter's day when it will be too cold to spend time there comfortably, but this is the reality of living with the seasons. In any case, a true solar space should always have the smell of the outside air and the character of external materials.

cool space

Conservatories can get very hot in the summer months. One way to drop the temperature is to create shade, either by growing creeping vines (left) or by installing conservatory blinds (above).

AN INDOOR GARDEN

Suffused with light, conservatories are ideal spaces for growing plants. As well as stimulating your senses by providing colour and perfume, plants can help to absorb certain pollutants in the home (see page 31, Chapter 2), purify the air by replacing carbon dioxide with oxygen and also provide your home with salads, fruits and herbs.

People
and pets

While eco-ideas work across generations, we are all individuals with differing needs. We age, acquire new things, share, meet a partner, have a child perhaps, discover new abilities and new disabilities, grow older than our bones might wish, move from the city to the country and then back again. Each change brings with it a new challenge, and the possibility of enriching our lives through careful choices. To make an ecofriendly home you therefore need to consider designs that work across generations, that can adapt to change without becoming obsolete or unwanted. Choose furniture and fittings designed for all and remember that your home will need to cope with many eventualities from home-working and child-care through to helping the old or the sick.

Chapter Five

Babies

As every parent knows, babies are affected by the world around them long before they are born: the chemicals in the air and in our food all affect the nurturing environment that is the womb.

To give your baby the best start in life, avoid smoky environments and remove heavily processed food from your diet. You should also take advantage of the nesting instinct by researching local sources of second-hand baby furniture and clothes and by preparing an ecofriendly nursery.

WHICH ROOM IS BEST?

Careful consideration is required when choosing a room in your home for your baby's nursery. It should be warm and cosy with enough space for a cot, clothing and a place to change nappies. Ideally, the room should be big enough so that the cot can convert into a bed for a young child. Choose neutral colours that won't overwhelm your baby and concentrate colour and sound in simple playthings that are safe to leave in the cot or suspended overhead instead.

Newborns cannot regulate their body temperature, so it is very important to make sure that the nursery has a good supply of heat (room temperature should be a uniform 18 to 20°C), with draught-free windows and heavy curtains or blinds that also serve to cut out

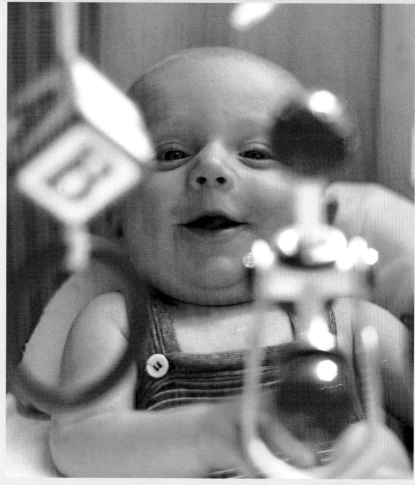

∧ **simple delights**
Babies are very easily amused, so entertain them with whatever it is you have to hand. Mobiles are an old favourite and you can even make your own with brightly coloured objects that vary in shape and form.

light. Since babies are highly sensitive to changes in light, a dimmer switch is ideal for the nursery. Alternatively, use lampshades to create soft, unobtrusive lighting. All electrical and gas fittings should be well maintained, so make sure that any old fittings, plugs and appliances are checked by a qualified electrician or plumber.

If you are intending to redecorate the nursery, consider choosing a chemically inert paint (see pages 67–8, Chapter 3), and remove fitted carpets to reduce the amount of trapped dust and house-bugs.

EQUIPPING THE NURSERY

Newborns grow very quickly so a lot of baby furniture is only used for a limited period of time. This is one very good reason to use secondhand furniture made from ecofriendly timber.

If you do buy new furniture, make sure you choose objects that are made from natural materials. Also, look for furniture that grows with your baby, rather than sits unwanted in the attic after only a few months of use.

Another option is to adapt existing furniture to suit the nursery, rather than buying items specially designed for your baby. A set of drawers with a mat and side rails on top, for example, can easily be used to store baby-changing essentials. A comfortable low chair can be moved from the living room into the nursery for breast-feeding, and place simple wool rugs with non-slip backing strips on the floor to let your baby toddle around in comfort.

Similarly, be creative with other baby paraphernalia. Rather than buying a special sterilising appliance, just sterilise bottles using a saucepan with a lid.

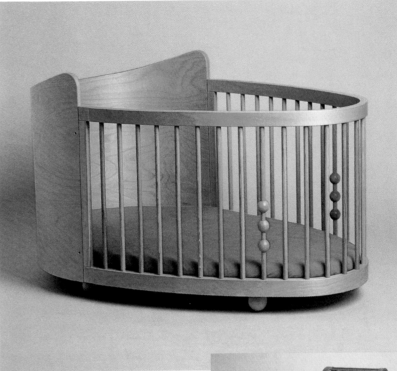

functional furniture
This timber cot can be dismantled after the first year to create a chair with adjustable seating and an indoor climbing frame. An additional piece of wood creates a slide.

BABY TOYS
There are two approaches to buying baby toys. The first is to buy them as an instantaneous amusement fix, and the second is to buy them with a view to them becoming treasured objects that last a lifetime and beyond. Unaffected by the powers of marketing and advertising, most babies are at their happiest playing with simple household objects that create sound, such as jangling a set of keys, banging pots and pans with wooden spoons or crumpling up soft tissue paper or newspaper. The shop-bought, brightly coloured, noisy battery-run plastic contraptions will also keep your

< fun with food
Babies love playing with food, and will find great delight in helping you to prepare meals. Introduce your children early to the pleasures of fresh, organic produce and you will help them to establish a healthy attitude to food.

Eternally yours: the toy box

If this is your first baby, consider buying a large, solid wooden box to store all your children's toys. Not only will this serve its purpose during baby and toddlerhood, it will also be a useful piece of furniture for years to come. Use it to store linen, old files and anything else that you want to keep but don't need to hand. You can even make one yourself.

BABY CLOTHES

As babies grow very quickly, newborn clothes are only worn for a very short time. Friends and family who have already had babies are a good source of relatively new hand-me-down vests, babygrows, socks, mittens, baby bonnets and bibs, so make sure to ask them for any cast-offs before you splash out on a brand new baby wardrobe. Alternatively, keep your baby's clothes for your next baby, or offer them to friends who are about to start a family.

If you do buy secondhand clothes for your baby, choose ones that are made from natural materials, such as cotton, and make sure that they are free from chemicals. This will help to keep your baby's skin free from allergic reactions until she or he has built up a natural resistance to the world and its surroundings.

baby quiet but will, most likely, eventually end up in an unwanted pile somewhere, either broken or out-of-date. If you do decide to buy manufactured toys for your baby, look for well-made, solid, durable and imaginative items made from natural materials that can be dismantled easily. These can then become a set of building blocks as your baby's dexterity gradually develops.

∨ eco-toys

Always try to choose toys made from sustainable materials, such as wood, and make sure the paints used to decorate them are non-toxic. Soft toys should always have hypoallergenic fillings.

NAPPIES

One of the biggest questions with babies is whether you should buy disposables or join the cotton club. While the original cotton nappy was rough, bulky, leaky and hard to change, the modern equivalents are sleek, soft, watertight and use NASA-approved velcro for quick release. Some even have micro-fibre covers which allow your baby's skin to breathe.

Over the first two years of your baby's life, you will use at least 2000 disposable nappies, all of which are manufactured from highly treated cotton and plastic. They are bleached and, more recently, filled with chemically dubious liquid-absorbing gels, and are also difficult to dispose of safely. Reusable nappies, on the other hand, can last for a decade and, if washed in bulk and dried on the line, use less energy than the mass-marketed alternative. Better still, join a local nappy club that will collect your used nappies, wash them in bulk and return them clean weekly.

Midway between the two ends of the nappy war are the nappy kits that contain flushable (or compostable) liners, cotton nappies and waterproof pants. These are ideal for when you and your baby are travelling away from home.

MADE IN NORWAY

Adaptable chairs

Manufactured in Norway, these solid wooden chairs are made from cultivated beech. The height and depth of the seat and footrest can be adjusted, so they are ideal items of furniture for a growing child. The seat can elevate to the height of the table, ensuring that your children are sitting at the right height for the table with their feet supported at the same time. With extra cushioning and a safety harness, they make appropriate high chairs for babies aged between 6 and 12 months who can support their heads. The enduring quality of the wood means that teenagers and adults will also be able to sit comfortably on them.

Children

Once weaned, out of nappies and in their own room, kids are a bundle of laughs, frights, cares and despairs in equal measure. Between the ages of three and thirteen your children learn more about the world around them than they will learn in the rest of their lives. Many of these adventures and learning experiences will happen in the privacy of their own bedroom, away from the organising rigour and limiting imagination of parents. The key requirement for a child's bedroom is that it should be a haven for imagination and growth. However, you should also cover the practical matters of comfort and safety.

ALLOCATING ROOMS

Children will play, sleep, dress and do homework in their bedroom, so don't try to to squeeze them into the smallest room in your home. Where possible, choose a room that is large enough for all these needs or, if you have two or more children, consider giving them smaller sleeping rooms with a separate room to house all their toys and play with their friends.

For everyone's sake, a child's bedroom should be separate from the parents'. If you want to keep an ear on your kids when they are small, install a wire-free baby monitor in their room. Make sure you take it out before they realise that you're eavesdropping, by which time they'll be old enough to take care of themselves.

Safety first

From a safety point of view, you may want to choose a bedroom on the ground floor to reduce the danger of falling downstairs but, alternatively, a children's bedroom upstairs means you don't have to tiptoe around the house after early evening bedtimes. If you do opt for upstairs, make sure that you have a well-secured stair guard and that the surface you choose to cover the stairs isn't too slippery.

FURNITURE

Where possible, always choose over-sized furniture: big beds and chairs are great fun for kids because they provide far more opportunity for play than tiny

> **totally engrossed**
One of the joys of childhood is being able to live in a world of make-believe. As a parent, the benefit of this is that you don't have to buy the latest toys. With a little imagination (both yours and your child's!) simple, well-made toys provide just as much fun.

< **neutral colours**
Ideally, the colour scheme for a kid's bedroom should be pale or neutral because this will allow for more flexibility as and when your children's tastes develop and change.

bunkbeds are one good solution, but make sure the child in the bottom bunk can sit up comfortably without hitting the top bunk. Another separate but compact alternative is to screen off the area around the bed for some privacy, but maintain a common dressing and play area. This arrangement should work well until the teen years arrive.

DECORATIONS

A simple combination of colours and materials will provide a good backdrop for your kids' own imagination and endure the fads throughout the years.

When the time comes your children won't hesitate to plaster their bedrooms walls with their favourite pop and TV stars, but this is far better than imposing a colour scheme or heavily patterned

stools and cots. They'll also last longer and form part of your child's personal possessions as they grow. Timber makes warm and robust furniture, while steel tubular furniture with fabric covers is colder to the touch, but lighter and therefore easier to move around.

Obviously, the cupboards, desks and drawers you choose should be designed so they can actually be used by children, but consider building shelves, firstly at a low level, then adding upwards to match both your child's height and their increasing number of toys, clothes and books.

Colourful polypropylene storage boxes are light, cheap and sturdy, so are perfect for storing away toys at the end of the day.

For wardrobes, buy ones that close securely as this will protect clothes from dust and moths. They will also give your kids' rooms a semblance of tidiness.

At an early age, kids love to share their rooms with their brothers and sisters because it provides them all with security and play friends. But beyond the ages of eight or nine, they may start to want their own space and you will have to see whether your home can cope with the increased demand. If space is a problem,

> **soft edges**
The corners of tables and other sharp edges often fall at children's head height, so they may pose a danger. To avoid this, attach plastic corner bumpers.

design to the room, which will age even more quickly in a rapidly growing child's eyes.

Keep a cork pinboard on the wall to stick up favourite pictures or schoolwork and maybe keep another wall free for your children to paint however they feel suits them best each year. Blackboard paint on part of a wall is another good way.

Floors in a child's bedroom are best off being soft and easy to clean. Linoleum is preferable to fitted carpets and any rugs should have non-slip backing in order to prevent accidental slipping. For safety's sake, keep furniture away from window sills and install a window stop so that they can't

∧ **riding the wave of technology**
As your children grow older, they'll definitely want to be part of the digital age. In addition to being fun and educational, small portable computers also consume very little energy and space.

ECOTIP

Fostering awareness
As one environmentalist puts it, 'we do not inherit the earth from our parents, but borrow it from our children', and childhood is the time to encourage your children to think about cause and effect, particularly with regard to the environment. You can do this by planting a vegetable patch together and watching things grow, taking your children to the market and asking them to smell items to discover whether they are ripe or not, or buying them a bike so they can cycle to school.

---

open more than a hand's depth. Fabric roller blinds make good window screens and hold less dust and are less likely to be broken than wooden ones.

ECOLOGICAL TOYS

Any plaything that is adaptable, multi-functional, non-toxic, made from tough renewable materials and long-lasting so that it grows with your children can be considered an eco-toy. Unfortunately, many modern toys are designed either to be instant fixes or part of a collectable series that's fashionable this year but disappears the next. These encourage cupboards full of junk that nobody wants and a kid screaming out for more – not a pretty sight! The following are just some of the many eco-options, so set some basic parameters and see if your kids can lead the way!

Froebel toys
The German educationalist Friedrich Froebel created a series of eight gifts that formed a basic part of his 'earth-centred' educational ideas. The gifts start as simple playthings that help kids to see and understand basic shapes and textures like soft spheres and hard cubes, then grow into building blocks and frameworks, eventually becoming hobbies such as embroidery, modelling and mat-weaving.

Cut and paste
Kids love cutting out pictures from last week's magazine and pasting them into scrapbooks, so have a good supply of non-toxic glue, paints, pencils and scissors. Every time the old book runs out, buy a new one, and encourage your child to make collages of colour and do some play-writing in it

every once in a while. In years to come, these will serve as a diary of sorts that you and your kids can treasure. Similarly, set aside a box in which to keep old wrapping paper, egg cartons and toilet rolls and encourage them to make their own playthings.

Outdoor sports

Whether the preference is football, tennis, hockey or rugby, ball games keep your children fit. Encourage your children to invite friends over to play as this will help them to get out of the house and away from the TV. Sport has turned into big business, but all in all it is far better than war!

A bike is also a great idea and probably the first bit of freedom that a child can receive. If you are worried about the local streets being dangerous and polluted, then get complaining to your local council now and get your kids involved it in too!

> solar-powered
Buying radios and other electrical equipment that are powered by the sun will curb the need for disposable and non-recyclable batteries.

Electrical games

There are plenty of cautions that apply to this medium, but overall, it is possible to see the ecological benefits through the haze of mass consumer electronics. If you choose wisely, items such as an internet connected portable computer or solar-powered radio can provide hours of fun and learning without consuming vast amounts of energy or materials. In eco-design this is called dematerialisation – matter disappearing and being replaced by 'pure' communication.

Old favourites

Chess, scrabble, cards and dominoes are among the few

games that last forever, and are guaranteed to entertain and educate your children well into the teenage years and adulthood. If you can afford it, choose the well-made versions as these may even outlast your kids, who can give them to their own children.

< life-long pursuits
Give your children a means to focus their natural inquisitiveness by encouraging them to take up a hobby, such as learning a musical instrument.

Teenagers

By this time, your children will be independent, aware and often cranky. Everyone needs their own space and teenagers are no different. They also have their own ideas of how space should be decorated and maintained. Some teenagers are clumsy, messy and liable to break anything that moves. Others are tidy to the point of neurosis. Most, however, fall somewhere between and could do with some help in deciding how to furnish their rooms.

NECESSITIES

As well as reflecting his or her general taste, a teenager's bedroom should have adequate space for studying. This means a desk (preferably with drawers), a comfortable chair and lots of shelving for storing books.

Teenagers will want to use their rooms to entertain friends, so make sure there is enough space for this. A low bed is good for lounging on, but consider also large floor cushions or bean bags.

Choose well-made, tough furniture that is also mobile and loose-fitting. This allows them to move things around as their needs and tastes change. You may be able to buy well-made desks at knock down prices from schools or offices that are refurbishing. Also, consider that your teenage children may take their bedroom furniture with them when they leave home. To make sure they will be happy doing this, discuss choices together and involve them in the purchasing process.

Listening to loud music is an inevitable part of teenage life, so for everyone's sake, make sure your teenager's room is well insulated. If there is space, build cupboards either side of the door. Filled with books and other belongings, this will act as an acoustic barrier between their room and the rest of the house.

If the room has enough height, you can build a high-level platform for a futon or mattress and the space underneath can act as a work or music den. Alternatively you can use this space for extra storage.

< peace and privacy
Teenagers will invariably spend hours chatting on the telephone, so make sure they have the comfort, privacy and means to do this in their own bedrooms.

Young adults

During our 20s, most of us are determined to work hard and play hard, which leaves little time to think about the damage we wreak on the environment. Food is fast, convenient and throw away; fashion is up-to-date and disposable; and furniture is cheap, cheerful and short-lived. However, living in tune with the planet doesn't mean dropping out of this modern lifestyle. All we need to do is look before we leap.

FURNITURE

Most of our furniture requirements are just as appropriate when we are young as when we are old. But we do need to pay extra attention to certain matters at this stage in our lives. Because we are often on the move, the best way of making things last is by purchasing small, portable and tough furniture that we can lug from place to place with relative ease. However, this doesn't have to mean uncomfortable or plain; a multi-coloured wool rug can be rolled up and lain out anywhere. Futons and timber bases can be re-arranged a dozen times to function as bedding, coffee tables or a couch. Equally, don't be caught up in convention: stack a pile of totally unrelated secondhand shelves on top of each other and fill them with your favourite things. As well as being a cool composition of your own, this will

∧ flat sharing

Getting a job and moving out of the parental home combine to make the early 20s an incredibly exciting time. Make a habit of shopping and cooking together because it's cheaper, more fun and will save energy too.

be as cheap as poorly made furniture and last far longer.

ECOLOGICAL AWARENESS

If you are renting, it is unlikely that you'll be able to afford, let alone feel responsible for, improving the energy efficiency of your home over the long term. Despite this, you can undertake very simple measures to do your bit for your home and the planet. Draught-stripping, installing temporary cling-film double glazing and buying low energy bulbs that you can take with you are all cheap and easy and will decrease your utility bills. Instead of turning up the thermostat on cold, wintery days, get in touch with the seasons and wear socks and an extra jumper instead. Whenever you leave a room, remember to turn off the lights and whenever you go away for the weekend, turn off the heating.

Later life

It is only when we reach our later years that we discover the worth of our possessions. As we look back on our lives, we find that the things we treasure most are simple and long-lasting – friends, a perfect view, memories of life events, a favourite record or a tree planted 40 years ago that is now grown and gnarled.

Reflection also involves looking around you at the big house you have grown used to over the past years, the rooms where children have played and screamed, the double garage, and the neat suburban neighbourhood that many of us will find ourselves in. Looking towards the future includes dealing with retirement when our incomes will fall, the prospect of grandchildren and, let's be honest, facing the onset of frailty and our eventual demise.

DOWNSIZING

When the children have flown the nest, it is time to reconsider your household needs and desires, and repackage yourself so that you can really do more with less.

For some, downsizing involves selling the big family home with the big energy and maintenance bills, and finding a smaller dwelling. Perhaps a small pad in the city where you can entertain and maintain it with ease. If the city smog is getting you down and green fields beckon, find a cottage in your favourite small village, where the post office and the pub are still going strong.

When your home no longer supports a growing family, this is the time to replace large-scale, energy-consuming appliances, such as an Aga, with those that are designed for just one or two. In essence, aim to reconfigure your life so that it flows with the world around you.

> **low maintenance**
Once children leave home, a large lawn may not be so important, so consider a courtyard with wood decking instead.

> special needs

This kitchen is specially designed to cater for those with reduced mobility. It features taps that are easy to turn on and off, low level sinks with wheelchair access and mobile storage units that also double as worktops.

For others, downsizing may simply involve a careful review of our daily habits. Good insulation and thick curtains will keep your heating bills low, as will turning down thermostats in unused rooms. Likewise, turning the lights off when they are not needed and using electrical appliances wisely will cut down on your electricity bills. Taking in lodgers is another way of ensuring that your home and its resources aren't wasted.

If you have the time, consider taking up a practical hobby, such as sewing or woodworking. This way you'll be able to take advice from your grandparents and make-do with mending.

CATERING FOR DISABILITY

Even if we are in good health, we should always consider the needs of others and make our homes more user-friendly for those who are less physically able. Many countries now have legislation for new housing to meet minimum standards of accessibility.

Basic requirements

One of the basic needs for disabled people is that there is enough space to move around key parts of the home in a wheelchair. For this reason, make sure doorways have flat or only slightly ramped access. They should also be at least a metre wide with a clear opening.

Any stairs in your home should have comfortable handrails beside them. A contrasting floor covering on each step will also mean that stairs are easily visible to those with poor eyesight.

Easy access to toilets and bathrooms is critical as it can take more time to reach these rooms if you are less steady on your feet. If possible, have a toilet on each floor of your home, particularly the ground floor.

Facilities in the bathroom should include a wide shower space with a tip up seat, an adjustable shower head and vertical and horizontal handrails for support.

As we grow older, our joints may become stiffer and our muscles will grow weaker. To accommodate this, replace soft, low slung easy chairs with firm chairs that have straight backs. Taps with lever arms will also be easier to use than those with more traditional screw fittings.

< less is more

Later life is the time to downsize, so if you are still driving a spacious, gas-guzzling car, consider alternatives, such as the high-efficiency 'smart' car.

Pets

Not only are pets good companions, they keep us in touch with nature by the simple act and pleasure of caring for another creature. Despite this, they are not a simple option in an ecofriendly home and the larger they are, the more space, care and attention they need.

SPACE CONSIDERATIONS

Only choose a large pet, such as a dog, if you have plenty of space in your home and, ideally, a large backyard. You will also need to have time available to give them free access to the outside world because, just like humans, dogs will get bored of their own four fences. In comparison, cats make better pets in an urban environment as they are more able to care for themselves and less likely to be upset when left to their own devices.

Smaller pets, such as hamsters and rabbits, are normally kept in cages to prevent them from getting lost or fouling the home and, as a result, they live a dull and mundane existence in a trapped environment. You and your children may think they are cute and entertaining, but they really would prefer to be out there in the big wide world, and for this reason, they are not recommended.

A more ecological approach to pets is to keep them for their usefulness. Chickens, for example, will happily eat most kitchen scraps as well as produce eggs and

˅ **clean and happy**
Teach your children to wash their hands and faces after handling pets and opt for wood flooring rather than carpets because these are easier to clean.

< **faithful companions**
If you live on your own, caring for a pet can give you a sense of purpose and belonging. Cats make good pets in cities because they are independent and don't need much space.

over-the-counter medication, you may want to ask your vet about complementary pet medicine.

PET FOOD

The majority of pet food comes from industrialised slaughter houses, and it seems quite irrational of any owners who love their pets to feed it on the output of these. There are plenty of alternative cereal and nutrient-based pet foods, which are not only much better for your pets' digestion but also better for the environment in general. If you want to take pet food a step further, make your own from dining table leftovers.

manure. A tethered sheep will keep your lawn trimmed beautifully and provide an annual fleece of wool, while a pond filled with carp will stimulate a complex water eco-system and encourage a balanced mix of pond life.

HYGIENE
CONSIDERATIONS

Most pets are relatively clean by their own nature. However, they aren't as careful or as discriminating as we might hope and a home that includes a pet will undoubtedly require more cleaning than a home without. To make the task a little easier, choose wall and floor coverings that are easier to clean (see pages 56–64, Chapter 3).

> **lifestyle-compatible**
If there is little space in your home or you don't have a lot of time to care for one, you should choose a low maintenance pet, such as a goldfish.

Homes with pets will also have a greater risk of infestation from pests, such as fleas, mites and ticks. To avoid pet-derived illness, train your children to wash their hands and faces after playing with their pets, and regularly check both your children and your pets for signs of bugs, fleas and other undesirables. If your pet's infestation doesn't clear up with

Allergies

At some point in their lives, one in ten people will suffer an allergy. This is when the body's defence mechanism becomes hypersensitive and forms antibodies against a substance that is innocuous to most people.

DIFFERENT ALLERGIES

There are three different types of allergies: air borne, contact and food allergies. Air borne allergies are caused when we breathe in air that contains small dust or pollen particles or chemicals released by both natural and synthetic materials. Contact allergies are skin reactions to materials as diverse as the copper and nickel found in coins and jewellery, to synthetic chemicals such as formaldehyde, epoxy resin or thiurma that is found in cosmetics, rubber and reconstituted wood.

Scientists believe that most people will eventually react adversely to the chemically complex soup that makes up the modern living and working environment. By removing problem materials from the home and workplace, we can minimise this chance. Yet, concern for an allergy-free environment should not become an unhealthy obsession. Instead, aim to create a balance between accepting the world around you and combating realistic polluting sources.

PREVENTING ALLERGIES

To reduce the risk of developing or suffering from an allergy, aim to create a dry, dust-free and well ventilated home. Remove carpets and opt for hard flooring instead. To prevent dirt and dust accumulating in the home, wipe floors down regularly with a slightly damp cloth, close windows facing onto polluted streets and take off your shoes at the front door. Since damp air and surfaces are a haven for microbes, make

ECOTIP

A night in the cooler
Some experts believe that the common house mite is the cause of over half of all asthma cases. As tiny as grains of sand, dust mites thrive in bedding and carpets by feeding on sloughed off human skin cells that accumulate there. The Scandinavians get rid of these bugs by washing and drying bedding, then hanging it out to air for the night. The freezing temperatures kill the mites and in warmer climates the same results can be achieved by putting your pillow and duvet covers in the freezer overnight.

sure you address any damp problems in your home (see page 31, Chapter 2). In wet and humid climates you may have to buy a dehumidifier to deal with excessively damp air. You can also install a whole-house heat recovery ventilation unit to filter home air and reduce dust and chemical build-ups (see page 40, Chapter 2).

Choosing solid timber furnishings instead of heavily upholstered alternatives will also help, as will regularly washing fabrics and throws. Avoid having flowers, trees and plants that are pollinated by the wind, such as daisies, marigolds, willows and birch, near your home and select instead plants pollinated by insects and birds, such as fruit trees, sweet smelling flowers and herbs.

Since homes are becoming increasingly airtight, it is also very important to select general household materials and cleaning products that are beneficial or neutral to your health. For more information on ecological cleaning products see page 165, Chapter 6.

∧ **simple measures**
One way to avoid allergies is to keep plants in your home that are pollinated by birds and insects, such as herbs and fruit trees, rather than those that are pollinated by the wind.

< **clean and hypoallergenic**
Dust and house mites thrive in bedding, so change your sheets regularly. Using fabrics that are hypoallergenic will also help to prevent allergies.

Upkeep

Literally and figuratively, the home is a protective and nurturing
shell, and how we care for it has a direct bearing on how we care
for ourselves and our planet. Each layer of the home – from its
structure, insulation and utilities to the personal possessions inside
– can and should be maintained in an ecological way that improves
the health, quality and feel of our space and therefore our own
general wellbeing. Consider the three Rs (reduce, reuse, recycle) and
learn to spot potential problems before they envelop you.

Chapter Six

Maintenance and repair

The usual response to maintenance is a groan at the time, effort and expense involved, but each time you discover a problem try instead to see it as an opportunity to improve your home. Don't just make do and mend, think the problem through and devise a better, longer-lasting solution. A window is old and leaky, but has a great view into your garden. Maximise this by replacing it with a modern double glazed, timber-framed french window that opens onto the garden. Not only will you be replacing the window, you will be creating an alternative route outside and increasing the amount of light in your home. By improving as you maintain, you'll find the whole home maintenance experience much more rewarding.

OUTSIDE THE HOME

The ground outside your home can pretty much look after itself provided that it is well-drained and stable. Keep outside drains clear to prevent flooding and get a plumber to inspect manholes every few years to check that the brickwork down there is still sound. Similarly, if you plan on doing a lot of digging in your garden, take care because underground cables and pipes are often poorly marked and if you accidentally damage them, there may be disruptive and dangerous consequences.

Drainage

If the area around your home becomes waterlogged after heavy rains, this means your drainage is either blocked or inadequate. To improve drainage, either increase the size and number of drains around your home or create drainage channels at ground level which will draw rainwater away from the foundation walls. On larger properties you can even build a pond or water meadow to collect excess water. At the same time you will be creating an ecologically valuable and beautiful habitat. A landscape gardener or civil engineer will be able to run through all the options with you.

If you live in a particularly wet climate, place a border of hard, well-draining bricks against the side of your home. This will be a practical and attractive solution

∧ planning prevention pays

Like people, buildings can either grow old gracefully or fall apart at the seams rather disgracefully. Whatever you do, don't skimp on maintenance because it doesn't get any easier and the longer you leave it, the worse it gets.

and will work much better than poorly draining flower beds.

Tree maintenance

Above the ground, prune tall trees to prevent them from becoming too top-heavy and toppling over in high winds. Trees that are not on your property but whose branches hang over your side of the fence should also be tackled. In general, tall trees close to your home are best avoided because their roots burrow deep in search for water and can eventually cause damage to the foundations.

If your home is built on clay soils (ones that absorb water and expand or contract when dry) then trees growing close to your home will be even more of a problem. Broad-leaved trees or trees that grow quickly require a lot of water and consequently grow large root balls that spread outwards in search of water. You can't necessarily tell which trees cause a problem so monitor the garden and walls for signs of movement and call in a building surveyor if you are concerned. Large or older trees sometimes have preservation orders so you may have to ask your council for permission to remove dangerous trees or pollard them (see ecotip box, right).

Subsidence

If you notice cracks in the external walls of your home, this may be a sign of subsidence caused by shrinking soil or weak foundations. Underpinning, which comprises digging down to the base of the foundations and providing additional support, is expensive but a necessary measure if soil movement around your home is substantial.

PROTECTING YOUR FRAMEWORK

Rain, wind and sun are all pernicious forces which, unmanaged, can do great damage to your home. Rainwater can seep in unnoticed, rotting wood or rusting steel. High winds can destroy a poorly constructed home, tearing away weather-boarding and ripping up poorly fixed tiles. The sun heats up surfaces, making them expand and contract every day and night,

∧ pruning
Regularly lop off the branches from tall trees so that leaves and twigs don't find their way into gutters and drainpipes.

which affects surrounding materials and can eventually weaken and damage the underlying structure, allowing water and air to leak inside.

Gutters and downpipes

To protect your home against water damage, check and clear rooftop gutters and downpipes twice a year. Even if there are no tall trees near your house, birds may decide to make a sheltered gutter into a nest and cause blockage. See that gutters are still firmly secured to roofs and that pipes are securely bolted to the wall of your home. Roof tiles, flashing and also ridge tiles should also be checked at least once a year to see if there are any cracks or drips. At the first sign of damage, fix the problem. Otherwise it will grow

---

ECOTIP

Stemming tree roots
One way to prevent trees from damaging your house is to pollard them. This common procedure stops the root balls of trees from growing by cutting its branches back to the trunk. A pollarded tree grows straight, thin branches that can be used to make fences or provide renewable heating in the countryside.

> weekend chores
Leaves and other garden mulch will trap water and create damp, so regularly sweep or rake up around the outside walls of your home to keep them clear.

exponentially until you have no choice but to repair it and by that stage it will usually be at a high cost. If your gutters do need replacing, choose polypropylene piping as this is cheaper and longer lasting than metal or timber alternatives. You can also cover gutters with wire mesh to prevent leaves from falling in. While you're at it, connect the guttering to a tank and reuse this water in and around your home.

Paintwork

Most external timber and metal work needs re-painting every five to ten years to protect it from the elements. Wooden window and door frames, external weather boarding and fascia panels are all vulnerable to the elements and should be checked yearly for signs of peeling paint, warping or rot. When it is time to repaint, consider whether a colour change might improve the feel of your home and neighbourhood (see page 66, Chapter 3).

External walls

Solid brick walls will also suffer from driving rain and cold temperatures, so examine these to check that the mortar is still filling the brick joints cleanly. If mortar is crumbling away, you will need to repoint the brickwork.

To prevent small repair jobs turning into major undertakings, always keep an eye out for any signs of damage. In particular, check that walls are straight, there are no cracks in the plaster and that roof lines are not sagging. If you have spotted signs of wear and tear, ask a surveyor or engineer to examine them further because they may be signs of more serious, underlying problems, such as structural damage.

Problems can also arise if you take down walls or use furniture or floor coverings that are heavier than originally intended. Never make holes in external walls without seeking the advice of a professional and only remove internal walls if investigation shows that it is neither supporting weight from above or stabilising the building. Check that joists and walls can support the extra load from heavy furniture, such as pianos or chunky flooring like terrazzo. If you find you do need to reinforce floors or walls, use secondary timber joists in preference to steel beams.

UTILITIES

Electricity, plumbing and gas are the hidden essentials of your home. When they fail you can end up with bills that far exceed the cost of maintaining them so consider these invisibles in your home maintenance programme.

Electricity

Its hard to be prescriptive about electrical systems as standards and regulations vary from country to country. However, aim to minimise your demand by choosing low energy appliances. This will also take some of the strain off cabling, fuses and power companies.

In older homes, cabling may be single-core with a lead or rubber sheath, while appliance flexes will be twin core twisted cables with no earth protection. All these wires need replacing professionally as they are dangerous and could lead to fire or electric shock. If fuses or circuit breakers continuously blow for no apparent reason, you are either overloading the circuit or the cabling is damaged. Tell-tale signs include warm cabling or a distinct fishy smell; you should either replace cabling or call in a qualified electrician.

When you move into a new property, you should always arrange to have electrical installations inspected to check and replace defective cables. A qualified electrician will also be able to check for damage caused by pests (who chew through cables), broken or burnt out sockets, unsheathed earth cables and overloaded circuits. Currently all domestic cabling in the UK is carried in PVC sheathing, which gives off toxic fumes when burnt. Alternative low smoke and flame (LSF) cabling is more expensive but is already commonly used in offices and will make a safer installation in your home.

Annual maintenance measures you can do yourself include checking that fuses or circuit breakers in your distribution board are clean and operate properly, that plugs, appliance and lighting flexes don't appear damaged, and testing and recharging batteries in smoke and carbon monoxide detectors.

Plumbing

Home plumbing is a major source of intermittent expense usually caused by accidental damage or ignoring obvious problems such as freezing pipes or dripping taps. If you do notice signs of leaking, always ring the plumber straight away rather than hoping the problem will suddenly disappear because it won't! In any case, it's a good idea to call a plumber to your home every five years or so so that he or she can pressure test the heating and water systems and identify any leaks or weak fittings.

More regular checks that you can carry out yourself include making sure that the insulation on water pipes is a minimum 25 mm (1 in), particularly in cold lofts and basements. If you need to apply or replace the insulation, choose the more eco-friendly alternatives of cork or mineral wool insulation instead of foamed plastics. If you live in an older home, ring your local council and ask them to conduct a water quality test to check that any lead piping has been replaced.

If pipework does need changing, use plastic fittings (polypropylene can be used for both hot and cold systems) which are cheaper, longer lasting and less toxic than metal alternatives. If you fit plastic pipes between metal fittings, you must also install an earth bonding cable to conduct electrical charges to earth. To save energy, add thermostats and timer controls to heating systems while they undergo maintenance work.

In hard water areas, limescale can build up inside water fittings, causing furring and eventual blockage. To prevent or remove limescale in your heating system, you will need to use a scale inhibitor, which you can buy in your local hardware store. Use

∧ **clean and efficient**
To remove limescale, dismantle and leave all tap parts in a bowl of vinegar or lemon juice overnight. Rinse and refit the following day.

lemon juice to remove limescale from shower heads by pouring the juice into a plastic bag and tying this around the shower head and leaving overnight. Citric acid crystals, which are available from chemists, are another option. A final ecofriendly option is to place magnets on either side of a hot water pipe. This will deactivate the lime scale particles and prevent future build ups.

Avoid blockages by putting a bin next to the toilet for sanitary towels, nappies and other toiletries and by using strainers in basin and sinks. Never pour paints or fats into the drains. Instead, pour them into a jar and reuse them. Alternatively you can pour them onto some old newspapers and throw the soaked newspapers in the waste bin.

To unblock toilets, fill a bucket of water and stand on a seat so that you can pour it from high level into the bowl. The force and quantity of the water should be enough to dislodge the blockage. If this doesn't work, pour boiling water into the bowl to soften or dissolve the waste matter, then use a plunger to force it clear.

Every now and again, fill bucket after bucket with used bath water and pour it down the loo. Bleach can be used as a final resort but choose the safer bleaches, such as hydrogen peroxide instead of normal household bleach, because its active ingredients disperse quickly in the environment. Never mix household chemicals in an attempt to double the strength because they may react together to create toxic fumes.

Gas

All gas-fired heating and cooking equipment needs regular maintenance to ensure that it is both safe and running efficiently. Most utility companies provide annual maintenance contracts and this includes checking that your systems are working properly. Gas appliances need to burn correctly

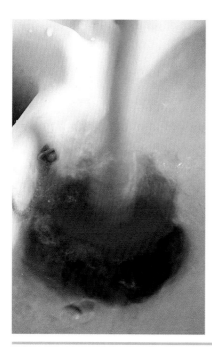

< fixing blockages
In place of expensive, strong chemicals that are dangerous as well as polluting, simply use a plunger or hot water to remove blockages in your sink or toilet.

∧ gas safety
Carbon monoxide alarms fitted next to gas appliances warn you of inadequate ventilation or damage to the burner. They can be bought from hardware shops.

and require effective ventilation to ensure that carbon monoxide does not build up in your home.

Gas burners need to be cleaned regularly as deposits will build up slowly and reduce the efficiency of the burner, leading to wasted energy. Maintaining your boiler will save as much energy as draught proofing doors and windows. Also check that plants are kept away from the boiler flue as this can also cause poor burning or create a fire.

If replacing your boiler, choose a high efficiency condensing type which can achieve heating efficiencies close to 95 per cent, particularly if you are running the system at low temperatures.

Household
cleaning

Cleaning shouldn't be an exercise in germ warfare and, contrary to popular belief, a spotlessly clean home has the potential to be just as bad for us in the long run as a home with a little dust and the usual signs of human life. It's common knowledge that kids fare better if they grow up surrounded by other children with a rich mix of germs and illnesses as this helps them to develop strong immune systems that will fight against future infections. Rather than 100 per cent sterility, create a naturally healthy environment in your home that is easy to clean with simple, non-toxic products.

FLOORS AND COVERINGS

Obviously, the type of floor you are cleaning will dictate the type of method you need to adopt. But, ultimately, you should be aiming to avoid getting your floors dirty in the first place. You can do this by using a big coir mat at the entrance of your home, taking shoes off at the front door and keeping spaghetti bolognese away from the carpet.

Wooden floors

A soft broom will remove most dust on wooden floors and a damp cloth will take care of the rest. If you follow a no-shoes policy in your home, you can even give your guests thick socks to walk around in and they'll polish your floor for free!

If your floors are sealed with linseed or wood oil stains, you will need to treat them again when the oils wear through, and if they are unsealed, polish them every year

CLOSE-UP: NATURAL WAXES

Waxes, oils and thinners are produced naturally by trees and bees (and even in our ears) or can be synthesised from petrochemicals. Beeswax, tung tree oil, linseed oil, gum tree turpentine and citrus peel oil are relatively safe, while oil derived products like paraffin wax, xylene and toluene are produced in high energy processes with complex waste products. Beeswax is a good all round polish which is easy to apply when thinned with medical grade white spirit (the least toxic thinner available). You can also turn it into an effective wooden furniture cleaner by mixing it with vinegar.

or so with a good beeswax polish. Avoid using scrubbing brushes on wood floors as the scratches increase the amount of dirt that collects on the surface. You should also avoid polyurethane varnishes which contain polyisocyanates as these can cause irritation or allergic reactions. Only polish or refinish when it is really needed.

Concrete floors

If it is to remain clean, bare concrete needs to be sealed, which can be achieved by polishing with wax or sealing it with a paint or

> smooth sailing
Hard flooring need only be swept and washed with warm soapy water to stay clean. Avoid strong cleaners or rough scrubbing brushes as these can pit or scratch the surface.

resin finish. Even low odour resins give off toxic gases, so apply them in summer when you can open doors and windows to evaporate the solvent. Several layers of wax are needed to take away the hard edge of untreated concrete but eventually it will glow warmly as it reflects the light.

Brick floors

If your hard floor is made of brick, it's best to allow the bricks to age naturally rather than plasticising them with uncharacteristic sealants. Glazed tiles, mosaics and terrazzo can be left unsealed or treated with resin sealants, while unglazed tiles and slates can be polished with linseed oil and beeswax. Use rugs on hard flooring to keep your feet warm or provide slippers for house guests.

Soft floors

Linoleum, cork and other soft resilient floors need a gentle sweep and a light soapy wash to keep

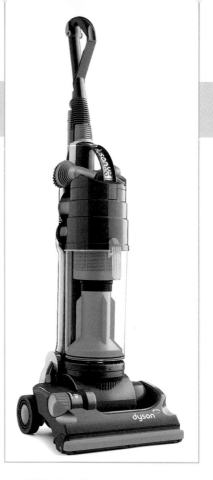

∧ HEPA filters
High efficiency particulate air filters remove up to 99.9 per cent of particles greater than 0.3 microns in diameter (a human hair is 100 microns thick), and can help in the fight against allergies.

them clean. You will find that linoleum lasts longer if it is polished occasionally.

Fitted carpets

These are literally the bug-bear for a clean home because they trap and hide dirt deep between the fibres. If you do have wall to wall carpets the best way to keep them dust-free is to clean them once a week with a high efficiency vacuum cleaner that has a ULPA or HEPA filter (see above).

For general carpet cleaning, dilute washing-up liquid with

warm water and whip the mixture up into a light foam with a whisk. Sponge the foam into the carpet and wipe with a damp cloth. Odours can be reduced in carpets by airing regularly and sprinkling with bicarbonate of soda followed, after a while, with a good vacuum. All carpets stain eventually, even those treated with proprietary stain guards, so have a set of stain removers on standby just in case.

Rugs

If you can manage it, rugs are best cleaned by shaking them outdoors. If you have a balcony, hang them over it and beat them with a traditional bamboo beater (a lightweight frying pan also works well). This cleaning method is often more effective than using a vacuum cleaner and airing the rug in the sunshine will also remove odours and kill house bugs. It also uses less energy, saves on vacuum bags and exercises your arms!

WALLS

Marks on painted walls can all be cleaned with a damp soapy cloth, unless the walls have a traditional lime white wash. This, if wiped can cause the mark to smudge. Because lime white wash is cheap and eco-friendly, the easiest way to clean these walls is by simply painting over any marks.

Dirt and grease from ceramic tiles in kitchens and bathrooms can be washed clean with a wet rag or sponge and some washing soda, a product derived from sodium carbonate that is relatively safe, cheap and readily available. Mould grows if you don't dry tiles after they get wet, and washing soda solutions will help to limit their growth. Make sure that corners and junctions are properly sealed using water-based acrylic sealants to prevent water damaging your building fabric.

Creating a healthy home (or a clean carpet at least!)

• Vacuum weekly with a high efficiency cleaner. If you have kids, make that twice a week.
• Make your home a shoe-free zone. Remove your shoes and you'll reduce harmful house dust by up to 90 per cent.
• Buy a coir door mat. Clean it weekly by taking it outside and banging it against the front wall. Don't deposit the dust over edible plants as it may contain lead and other toxins.
• Replace bare concrete outdoors with flower beds. These will help to absorb dust and pollution.
• Wash your hands before preparing or eating food. Kids always seem to have dirty hands and a quick wash before snacking should be an obligatory part of a healthy home.
• Don't smoke. That includes cigarettes, smoky fires and poorly maintained gas appliances. Yes, open fires are not healthy at all and are an inefficient way of heating your home.
• Avoid cleaners that contain toxic chemicals (see chart on page 165).

OTHER SURFACES

Water is nature's best solvent and most non-greasy dirt will dissolve or be washed away by a good douse of warm water. In many instances, simply wetting surfaces and containers and leaving them to soak will help to remove hard deposits. Grease doesn't dissolve in water so you will still need to buy soaps and other cleaners to clean things properly.

Cleaning products

While common household cleaning products have all passed various health and safety tests, many have been manufactured using dangerous industrial processes and are still not completely free of toxins. Chlorine and phosphate, two ingredients found in many common household cleaning products, pose particular threats: they create serious water pollution downstream from our drains or are toxic in contact with our skin. The eco-alternative is to clean your home with gentle and readily available products such as soap, soda, salt, warm water and some good old-fashioned elbow-grease.

KITCHEN CLEANLINESS

Food needs to be kept and prepared in a clean environment where chances of bacterial contamination are low. By their very nature, kitchens are also home to the toughest cleaning jobs with grease, oils and fats finding their way onto floors, work surfaces and ovens. But this doesn't mean you have to employ harsh cleaners containing toxic ingredients for the job. In fact, these products are just as likely to cause ill health as the bacteria they are designed to destroy.

You can clean most kitchen surfaces with soapy water and a little washing soda. A solution of washing soda or bicarbonate of soda, which is sponged down with clean water will do the job for fridges and ceramic tiles, while diluted vinegar cleans glass and descales kettles. Squeezing a little lemon juice onto a cloth, rubbing this into the stain then wiping clean removes most stubborn stains and heat marks on metal and melamine worktops.

Keep ovens clean by putting tops over your casserole dishes. Once you have finished cooking, coat the wet greasy hob surface with bicarbonate of soda and salt to make it easy to clean the next time. Sprinkle Borax powder in your bin to get rid of odours.

Shiny metal surfaces

These have become a popular look in kitchens in recent years, but involve a great deal of cleaning to >

< appreciating tarnish
Developing an eye for this beauty rather than the gleam of constantly polished silver or copper is one way to reduce pollution caused by the production and use of metal cleaning products.

HARMFUL HOUSEHOLD PRODUCTS AND THEIR ALTERNATIVES

We all aim to have homes that are clean and safe sanctuaries, but many common household products contain proven physical and environmental toxins, which can accumulate over time and cause serious damage to our health. Have a good look through your cleaning cupboards and replace these with the suggested alternatives.

Household products	Harmful ingredient	Alternatives
Batteries	Cadmium, mercury, nickel, sulphuric acid, zinc	Use rechargeable batteries or mains power
Bleach	Chlorine	Avoid bleaching or use hydrogen peroxide
Carpets	Butadiene, styrene, ethylbenzene	Choose natural rugs and avoid cheap foam underlays
Dyes	Ammonia	Use natural vegetable dyes
Deodorants	Ethylene glycol	Talcum powder
Dry cleaning/ fabric cleaner/ spot remover	Perchloroethylene	Avoid dry-cleaning fabrics
Lawn treatment	Chlorothanol	Hand pull weeds and plant camomile instead of grass
Mothballs	Napthalene, paradichlorobenzene	use lavender and cedar wood as repellents and keep cupboards closed
Air fresheners	Paradichlorobenzene	Avoid creating smoky atmospheres, ventilate rooms well and perfume with fresh cut flowers from your garden
Cleaners, polishers	Methyl ethylketone	Use beeswax or a half white vinegar, half vegetable oil mixture
Household plastics	Polyvinyl chloride	Use linoleum for floors and simple plastics such as polypropylene for containers
Toilet cleaner	Hydrochloric acid	White vinegar, lemon juice, baking soda, borax, washing soda, hydrogen peroxide

> maintain them. The strong chemicals in metal polishes are also toxic and it is possible to overpolish metal surfaces to the point of destruction. Instead, adopt the traditional Japanese approach by refraining from maintaining the newness of metal and allowing the layers of tarnish to slowly develop into their own rich patina.

If you still prefer the polished look, use home-made products instead of shop bought ones. To clean gold metals, mix equal measures of vinegar and baking soda in a jar and polish well. Use bicarbonate of soda powder with a little water to polish chrome objects and simmer silver items in a pot of water with aluminium foil and a tablespoon of washing soda.

Washing up liquids

The standard commercial dishwashing liquid is usually

phosphate-based, but the best eco-alternative is a vegetable-oil based detergent with salt and plant extracts. Ecover is just one organisation that makes alternative household products, washing up liquids included, which contain only botanical and natural ingredients. Buy them in bulk and reuse the containers for storing your own home-made house cleaning fluids. The other benefit of using vegetable-based dishwashing liquids is that dirty sink water can then be filtered and used to water the garden either directly or via a buried trickle hose. Alternatively use dirty water to soak pots and pans overnight.

Dishwashers

Older dishwashers use around 50 litres of water and therefore waste power and water. Modern energy-efficient ones can cope with 12 place settings (two to three day's washing), use less than 20 litres of water (the best use less than 15 litres), recycle heat between cycles and only use air to dry the dishes. Minimise the energy required by modern washing machines by supplying hot water direct from

< saving water

A standard kitchen sink holds between 10 and 20 litres of water and washing up after a family meal usually involves between 20 and 30 litres of water. An energy efficient dishwasher uses less.

your gas central heating, stacking the machine to its full capacity and using economy cycles. You can also save water by not using the prewash cycle: just dip dishes in a bowl of cold water after eating and this will stop deposits from drying in the first place.

If you don't have a dishwasher, then wash dishes in one bowl and rinse plates together in a second bowl of cold water. Leave pots to soak overnight with salt or potato peelings and wash them out with the next day's batch. Don't rinse under running water as this will waste buckets of water (literally!)

ECOTIP

Dry cleaning alternatives
The active ingredient in dry cleaning, perchloroethylene, is a carcinogen which causes reproductive, developmental and environmental damage, so its best to avoid clothes that need dry cleaning. In fact, many clothes labelled 'dry clean only' can actually be washed by hand; clothes manufacturers find it cheaper to write this on the label rather than test their clothing for washability. Consult a specialist cleaner who will be able to give you more detailed advice on clothes labelled 'dry clean only'.

REMOVING STUBBORN STAINS

The active ingredients required to shift stubborn stains can be found in a number of common household products so treat clothes with these before washing, instead of buying specific, heavy duty chemical products.

Stain	Method
Blood	Soak in cold water
Coffee and tea	Soak in solution of warm water and borax
Grass	Rub with glycerine
Ink	Rub with milk for fountain ink, turps for ball-points
Perspiration	Rub with clear vinegar
Tar	Rub with eucalyptus oil

WASHING CLOTHES

TV adverts implore us to wash our linens 'whiter than white'. But white never stays white for long and you could be forgiven for thinking that washing powder manufacturers encourage this behaviour for more than purely aesthetic reasons.

Apart from the environmental pollution caused by bleaches and other whiteners, there are plenty of good reasons to choose clothes that stay clean longer. The most obvious is the pleasure of not having to wash, dry and iron clothes every other day.

Most outer clothing stays clean for far longer than you imagine and sometimes all it needs is a night on the line to remove the odours from yesterday's smoky bar.

General dirt can easily be removed from clothes using a combination of two-third's soap flakes and one third bicarbonate of soda in a warm water wash cycle on your washing machine. Stubborn stains may need to be treated beforehand (see chart above). An alternative method is using ionising tablets that remove dirt in a washing machine without the use of conventional detergents.

Ionising tablets (or laundry disks) don't leave clothes smelling like 'fresh daisies' but they do clean well and only need recharging every sixty washes. You'll still need to use hot water on white clothing and treat stubborn stains beforehand but you'll save money, reduce the number of trips to the supermarket and have detergent-free cleaning that's gentle to sensitive skin.

Waste management

Cleaning and maintenance can create a huge amount of rubbish and manufacturers, shops and councils are all realising that waste is, well, a waste. Even so, we still seem to be filling bins at an inordinate rate of knots, throwing out nearly a tonne of rubbish from our homes each year.

While we all still produce waste, many environmental designers now believe that the future will truly be waste free. Instead of producing waste, we will hand on our unwanted resources to discard companies. We'll bundle them up at home to help the discard companies, who'll pick them up, clean them and sell them back to manufacturers as raw material. Plastics will go back to the bag man, metals to the tin-maker, glass to the bottle shop and much of the rest will be composted for our garden centres or burnt to produce heat and power. Discard companies will be hi-tech rag and bone men and the old saying, 'where there's muck there's brass', will never be truer.

In order to make this happen, we householders will have to learn to reduce waste to a minimum, reuse as much as possible and then choose things that can easily be recycled at the end of their lives.

RECYCLING

For household waste to be recycled it's important to buy products that have packaging which is easy to re-assemble. It is far easier to recycle a simple cardboard box, for example, than a plastic coated metal tin. Don't buy products that are packaged in complex containers, such as aerosols, air fresheners or oven cleaners, because more money goes into the can than into the product inside (it is even more of a waste when home-made products can do these job just as well).

You should also avoid buying dangerous and toxic products that will pollute the planet when discarded. If you can't avoid them then make sure that you dispose of them responsibly.

Set up a recycling cupboard at home. Old cards, paper and magazines can be used to soak up spillages, given to the kid's for painting and scrap-book making, or composted with garden and kitchen waste. Clean glass and plastic bottles and containers are good for mixing home-made

ECOTIP

Avoid in the first instance
To reduce the amount of housekeeping products that you use or buy, fill your home with possessions that do not require constant cleaning but actually wear well and look better as they age. Choose products that are long-lasting with minimal packaging and share or hire occasional items rather than buying them. A case in point is the average household drill, which, apparently, is only used for a half an hour in its lifetime!

for years before they wear down and have to be thrown out.

Composting

Twenty per cent of household rubbish comprises kitchen waste that can be composted and used as a free and effective fertiliser for your garden. You can make a compost area by putting a wire fence around a small corner of your yard or by buying a fixed or rotating compost bin from your local DIY store. Fill it with kitchen waste and garden cuttings and, in a few months, a rich mix of healthy garden food will appear.

To get good compost, layer dry material such as twigs between moist kitchen waste, add grass clippings to improve nitrogen content and insulate the pile with pieces of old carpet. Water occasionally to keep the area moist. Avoid adding animal or dairy fats as these decompose very slowly, encourage the growth of blue fly and attract scavenging animals into your garden. Once the waste has composted, spread it onto your garden as a mulch and let worms do the job of mixing the nutrients into the soil.

Wormeries

Compost bins can also be converted into wormeries. These produce a richer liquid garden fertiliser that can kick-start new plant growth without the need for chemical phosphates. To make a

worm bin, take a standard plastic composter and drill holes about 100 mm (4 in) from the bottom. Fill the bottom with gravel and water until it reaches the holes. Add kitchen waste, some manure and egg shells together with a handful of tiger worms (obtainable from an angling shop), then keep adding waste. The worms will multiply quickly and turn the compost into a very rich caste that you can mix with soil to produce excellent potting compost.

DISPOSING SAFELY

Quite a lot of our household waste is toxic which therefore needs to be disposed of carefully. Many local councils have facilities for handling toxic household waste and you should ring your local authority to find out more. Save up old oils, paints and pesticides and send them to your council's hazardous waste collection service. You can cut up unwanted leather and other textiles and use them as cloths or give them to charities. Take old medicines to your pharmacist for safe disposal.

Some products cannot be recycled so consider this when shopping. Disposable batteries, for example, add to waste fills, so always buy rechargeables or run electrical items from the mains.

cleaning products or for storing dried garden herbs. Cut plastic bottles in half and use them to protect growing plants in the garden. Tins and metal containers can be recycled into paint pots but make sure you file down any sharp burrs. In fact, most sensibly designed containers can be reused

Household pests

Not only do our homes provide a living environment for humans, they also attract a myriad of creepy crawlies. While some pests cause only mild irritation, others carry diseases and can turn our homes into a complete misery. There are plenty of commercial products on the market that claim to kill with just one quick spray, but this is because they are full of noxious substances that are also harmful to humans. Instead, make your home pest-free with simple physical barriers or natural pest repellents.

MOSQUITOES

Mosquito repellents, whether in sprays, coils or electric socket tabs, contain DEET, a chemical that is not only toxic to mosquitoes, but also to humans. While their use can be justified during a short trip to a hot climate, prolonged use is dangerous and unnecessary, especially when you can take alternative precautions.

In warm weather, mosquitoes can overwhelm the home, accounting for sleepless nights and itchy skin. In hot countries, mosquito screens across windows are almost obligatory and it is possible to make or buy similar screens in cooler regions. Where mosquitoes carry malaria, you should also use ceiling fans to stir the air, keep your skin covered, scent the air with citronella and use mosquito nets over beds at night. To reduce the number of mosquitoes in your garden remove all areas of still water, make sure your pond is aerated (a fountain helps to break up the water surface where larvae grow) and keep it well stocked with fish and frogs that eat growing larvae.

∧ **sleep well**
If you live in a hot and humid climate, mosquito nets are a necessity and are also much healthier alternatives to air conditioning and mosquito coils. Ceiling fans and open windows with insect-proof screens will help to create or let in cooling breezes.

MOTHS AND FLIES

These common visitors can often be found crawling around our wardrobes and kitchen cupboards where they lay larvae that chomp their way through natural fibres and food stores.

Moths

Napthalene or paradichlorobenzene are the active ingredients for mothballs and both are environmental toxins that alter natural ecosystems and destroy the balance between living creatures. Instead, control moths by keeping drawers, wardrobes and kitchen cupboards closed and regularly air the contents to check for signs of moth infestation.

Flies

Bluebottle and house flies are pests that are attracted to your home by rotting food and open food containers. Instead of reaching for the standard fly spray which, although an effective killer, contains harmful chemicals and artificial perfumes that are neither healthy or naturally biodegradable, avoid infestation in the first place. You can do this by covering food, clearing away leftovers straight away and generally keeping kitchens and dining rooms clean. Grow and dry fresh herbs in and around your home to scent the air and repel flies. Keep rubbish bins clean and site them as far from your home as possible.

FLEAS, ANTS AND COCKROACHES

Ants and roaches are attracted by open food, so again it is important to keep your kitchen clean. Sprinkle some boric acid (available from hardware stores) along ant trails to stop the path being reused and kill roaches by mixing equal parts of sugar and baking soda in a dish and placing this out of inquisitive children's reach. To prevent flea infestations, feed your pet tablets of brewers yeast and garlic and bathe them regularly during the flea season. You can also sprinkle your pet's bedding with fennel seeds and rosemary as the scent of these help to keep fleas at bay.

RODENTS

Rats and mice gnaw through unprotected timber, electrical wiring and plastic plumbing and find homes in crevices inside your walls or under the floor. If you suffer from rat or mice infestation,

< natural repellents
Dried lavender, orange peel and cedar wood chips release a scent that deter moths so place sachets of these in drawers to reduce infestation.

you need to close up any escape routes, such as holes in floorboards or skirting. While solid walls provide some protection, the best prevention is to store food and waste in sealed containers and to keep all surfaces free from food crumbs. If you keep a compost bin in the kitchen, make sure it has a secure lid to prevent smells from enticing vermin. Keep outdoor compost heaps away from the house and use a covered plastic or timber compost container rather than an open sided affair.

If keeping your kitchen clean doesn't do the trick, then lay down humane traps (boxes with a one way entry and a piece of food to entice rodents to enter) or get a cat to do the dirty work. Rat poison is a potential poison for small children and the standard spring-loaded death trap only adds to the chance of infection from rotting corpses hidden behind cupboards or under stairs. Rodents are also deterred by the strong scent of mint, so leaving sachets of mint leaves in your kitchen cupboards will also help.

Eco-rating guide

This final chapter provides an eco-rating for many of the materials and elements you are likely to find around your home. From the surfaces you stand on and lean against to the furniture you lounge on, how you use water and energy in your home, you will discover which are best suited to which areas of your home, for your health, for ease of maintenance and for the benefit of the planet. The ratings are as follows: 1 is excellent, 2 is average and 3 is poor; the lower the overall eco-score, the better the material or product. We have even taken price into account, so that saving the planet doesn't have to put a hole in your pocket.

Category	Energy consumption	Durability	Recyclability	Environmental pollution	Installation cost	Maintenance cost	Overall eco-score	Comments	Suitability
			Ecofriendliness						
Subfloor									
solid timber	1	1	1	1	2	2	8	Use local woods managed sustainably. Look for Forestry Stewardship Council (FSC) certification. Protect from damp. Can be used without further covering.	In wet rooms, protect with water-resistant covering.
concrete	3	1	3	2	3	1	13	Avoid on upper floors because heavy weight leads to complex structures that are difficult to change. Seal with low odour resins or cover with additional flooring. Use recycled aggregate (crushed concrete and stone) to reduce environmental impact.	Can help to reduce overheating in warm climates and will collect and store solar heat in cool climates.
Floor finishes									
Timber									
local hardwood	1	1	1	1	2	1	7	Good replacement for tropical hardwoods. Alder, ash, beech, birch, chestnut, elm, hickory, lime, maple, oak are all popular hardwoods.	Avoid in wet environments.
reclaimed wood	1	1	1	1	2	1	7	Reclaimed parquet is often cheap and in good condition. Wider planks are more expensive. Good types to use include mahogany or maple parquet, and old oak or pitch pine boards.	Avoid in wet environments.
tropical hardwood	2	1	1	2	2	1	9	Only use woods with Forestry Stewardship Council (FSC) certification.	Some woods, such as teak and greenheart, can be used in wet environments.
local softwood	1	2	2	1	1	2	9	Often cheap and plentiful, although less durable than many hardwoods. Good examples include pine, cedar, fir, larch and spruce.	

Category	Energy consumption	Durability	Recyclability	Environmental pollution	Installation cost	Maintenance cost	Overall eco–score	Comments	Suitability
	Ecofriendliness								
bamboo ply	1	2	2	1	2	1	9	Not strictly a wood, but preferable to other tropical plywood.	Can be used in bathrooms.
non-tropical plywood	2	2	2	2	1	2	11	Not as hardwearing as solid wood. Choose plywood with low odour resin content. Will need many coats of varnish to protect from damage.	Avoid in heavily used areas of the home and those that are likely to get wet frequently.
Soft flooring									
linoleum	2	1	2	1	1	1	8	This soft, warm and low-cost flooring is made from all natural ingredients and is available in plain and marbled finishes.	Good for all types of rooms.
cork	1	2	2	1	1	2	9	This is made from natural materials, bound with glues and baked to form tough tiles. Seal to avoid pitting.	Suitable for less frequently used rooms, such as the bathroom.
rubber	2	1	2	2	2	1	10	Made mostly from synthetic materials, rubber is mixed with ground stones and binders to make a long-lasting, water resistant material that can be dyed in many colours. Some manufacturers use recycled or natural materials.	Use in rooms that get wet often, such as bathrooms, kitchens and utility rooms.
vinyl (pvc)	1	2	2	3	1	2	11	This is made from a complex mix of PVC binders and plasticisers, which have known carcinogenic contents. Softer vinyls give off more pungent odours than harder tiles.	Avoid or use sparingly in rooms that get wet.
Hard flooring									
stone (slate, marble, granite, etc)	2	1	2	2	3	1	11	Strong and low maintenance, but expensive. Choose locally produced stones in preference to imported stock.	Use sparingly in rooms that are heavily trafficked or get wet frequently.

Category	Energy consumption	Durability	Recyclability	Environmental pollution	Installation cost	Maintenance cost	Overall eco-score	Comments	Suitability
	Ecofriendliness								
reconstituted stone	2	1	3	2	3	1	12	Made from ground stone and cement or resins. It has a lower environmental impact than raw stone because it uses waste products efficiently.	Use sparingly in wet environments and areas with heavy traffic.
ceramic	2	1	3	2	3	1	12	Made from glazed or unglazed fired clay that can be coloured with a variety of finishes.	Use sparingly in wet environments and areas with heavy traffic.
terrazzo	2	1	3	2	3	1	12	This mix of marble or glass is tough and long-lasting. If laid on site, sealants are unnecessary.	Use sparingly in wet environments and areas with heavy traffic.
brick	3	2	2	2	2	2	13	If possible, use reclaimed bricks to reduce energy consumption and lime mortar to allow easier recycling in the future.	Use externally or in semi-external situations.
metal flooring	3	2	1	2	3	2	13	Metal tile floors (including those made from aluminium and zinc) require a lot of energy for their production.	Avoid use if possible.
Floor coverings									
wool rugs	1	2	2	2	2	2	11	The more knots per inch, the tougher (and more expensive) they will be. Persian and Oriental rugs are particularly long-lasting.	Well-made rugs can be used throughout the home, but don't use in areas that are damp or have a lot of traffic.
cotton rugs	2	3	3	2	1	2	13	Lighter and less hardwearing than wool rugs. Most cotton is farmed irresponsibly so look for organic sources if possible.	Easily washable so suitable for use as mats in bathrooms.
fitted wool carpets	2	3	2	1	2	3	13	These are softer and more expensive than synthetic carpets.	A no-shoes policy in the house will increase its life and reduce cleaning costs.

Category	Energy consumption	Durability	Recyclability	Environmental pollution	Installation cost	Maintenance cost	Overall eco-score	Comments	Suitability
			Ecofriendliness						
natural fibres (seagrass, jute, sisal, hessian, etc)	3	2	1	2	2	2	12	These are generally less processed than carpets and use less intensive dyes.	Wears easily, so avoid in heavily trafficked areas.
fitted synthetic carpets	2	3	3	2	1	3	14	Nylon, acrylic and polypropylene carpets are not soft or hardwearing, but are cheaper than wool ones.	Avoid use when possible.
Carpet underlays									
felt	1	2	1	1	1	2	8	Ensure that this has adequate bounce to protect carpet from wear.	
recycled rubber	1	2	2	1	1	2	9	This has good eco-credentials, reducing carpet wear and noise transmission.	
sponge rubber	2	3	2	3	1	2	13	Many of these contain harmful organic chemicals and some are so soft that they crumble away after a few years.	
Internal walls									
timber stud and plaster-board	1	1	3	1	1	1	8	These are simple to construct and modify. Include cellulose insulation to increase sound insulation.	Suitable for all internal walls.
concrete block and plaster	2	1	2	2	1	1	9	Lightweight concrete blocks consume relatively little energy, but concrete walls are far harder to modify at a later date. To improve eco-credentials, use blocks made from waste materials, such as power station ash.	Only use on floors that have been designed to take the load.
brick and plaster	3	1	2	2	1	1	10	Brick is heavier and more energy intensive than lightweight concrete.	Avoid where possible.

Category	Energy consumption	Durability	Recyclability	Environmental pollution	Installation cost	Maintenance cost	Overall eco-score	Comments	Suitability
			Ecofriendliness						
Wall finishes									
wallpaper	1	2	2	1	1	2	9	A cheap and effective wall covering. Avoid vinyl wall paper because it doesn't allow the structure to breathe.	Avoid in wet rooms.
timber boarding	1	1	2	1	2	2	9	Use FSC certified softwood panelling.	Avoid in wet rooms to prevent rot.
cork	1	1	2	1	2	2	9	Cork tiles are tough and ecofriendly but can look dark and outdated.	Use in bathrooms or on walls used for posters or notes.
natural fibres	1	2	2	1	2	3	11	Paper coated with hessian, silk, wood veneers or dried grasses is less robust than printed paper but more interesting.	Use decoratively in living rooms and bedrooms.
ceramic tiles	3	1	3	2	2	1	12	Long-lasting, water resistant and available in many styles, sizes and colours.	Use in bathrooms, kitchens, utility rooms and hallways.
metal panelling	3	1	1	3	3	2	13	Easier to fix than ceramic tiles but less resistant to water damage.	Avoid or use sparingly in place of ceramic tiles.
Natural paints									
mineral	1	1	1	1	2	1	7	Based on waterglass (potassium silicate), this bonds deeply into plaster or concrete to create a long-lasting and colourfast finish.	Generally used externally on plaster but can also be used internally for solid colour and glazed finishes.
casein	1	2	1	1	2	2	9	This is distemper with the addition of a milk protein binder to make it tougher and longer-lasting.	Can be used throughout the home.

Category	Energy consumption	Durability	Recyclability	Environmental pollution	Installation cost	Maintenance cost	Overall eco-score	Comments	Suitability
			Ecofriendliness						
distemper	1	3	1	1	1	2	9	This is made from chalk, water and horn glue mixed together and coloured with natural pigments to create a grainy and soft surface that breathes well and glows in reflected light.	Suitable for plaster and woodwork that is far away from moisture and dirty hands.
Synthetic paints									
acrylic	2	2	3	2	1	2	12	Choose ones with low volatile organic compounds (VOC) to reduce environmental damage.	Can be used throughout the home, but natural paints are better.
high-sheen water based	2	1	3	3	2	2	13	These give off volatile organic compounds (VOC) that cause physical damage over a long period of time.	Use on woodwork or metalwork, but avoid indoors.
oil-based	3	1	3	3	3	1	14	As for high sheen, but with greater concentration of VOCs.	Use on woodwork or metalwork, but avoid indoors.
lead-based	3	1	3	3	2	2	14	Take care when stripping old paint which may contain lead.	Lead is a toxin and should be avoided in the home.
Furniture									
timber	1	1	2	1	2	2	9	Solid timber furniture is tough and long-lasting. Choose local hardwood timbers with solid joints and waxed surfaces.	Avoid using in rooms that get wet easily because wood eventually rots.
plastic	2	2	3	2	1	2	12	Cheap, but often poorly made. UPVC in particular ages poorly, especially when exposed to the sun.	If well-made, it will be tough so use outdoors or for children's furniture.
metal	3	1	1	3	3	2	13	Steel and aluminium are commonly used to make chair frames and cupboards. If well-made, they last a long time, but thinner metals often deteriorate quicker. Source recycled metals where possible.	Use sparingly around the home. Aluminium makes long-lasting garden furniture.

Category	Energy consumption	Durability	Recyclability	Environmental pollution	Installation cost	Maintenance cost	Overall eco-score	Comments	Suitability
	Ecofriendliness								
mdf/ melamine	1	3	3	2	1	3	13	Cheap, but short lived materials that are best avoided unless designed carefully.	Avoid in wet and fragile environments.
Lighting									
daylight	1	1		1	1	1	5	Enhance with light coloured surfaces. Reduce associated night time heat loss with curtains, aluminium blinds and high efficiency double glazing.	Promote daylight by opening curtains and turning off electric lights.
compact fluorescent	1	1	3	1	2	1	9	A wide variety of sizes and qualities available, varying from dull, insipid colour rendering and slow start to fast, small and mellow output.	Use for desk lamps and in ceiling shades. Choose warm colour rendering and instant-on bulbs for living spaces, and cheaper bulbs elsewhere.
linear fluorescent	1	1	3	1	2	1	9	Slim-line tubes are most efficient. Choose electronic ballast type for instant on and non-flicker effect.	Use in bathrooms, utility rooms and concealed above work surfaces in kitchens.
tungsten halogen	2	2	3	2	1	2	12	Small, punchy white light from low voltage lamps with transformers.	Good for spot lighting in kitchens and living rooms. Can also be used in appropriate desk lamps.
tungsten	3	3	3	3	1	3	16	Short-lived and high energy consumers.	Use sparingly with dimmer switches.
Ventilation									
passive stack ventilation	1	1		1	3	1	7	These small (4 to 6 in) tubes with humidity controlled dampers are good alternatives to positive extract ventilation.	Only use in bathrooms and kitchens when there is easy access to the roof directly above the room.
trickle ventilators	2	1		2	1	1	7	Simple but not particularly energy conscious.	Use in living rooms and bedrooms.

Category	Energy consumption	Durability	Recyclability	Environmental pollution	Installation cost	Maintenance cost	Overall eco-score	Comments	Suitability
	Ecofriendliness							Comments	Suitability
whole house heat recovery ventilation	1	2		1	3	2	9	Relatively expensive but if well designed with low energy fans and good controls, will reduce heating energy in well-sealed homes.	Often only appropriate in modern houses with tightly sealed windows. Consult a supplier for suitability.
positive extract ventilation	2	2		2	2	2	10	Choose quiet and efficient fans and use humidity controls.	Use in kitchens, bathrooms and utility rooms.
Electrical energy supply									
renewable utility company	1			1	2		4	These charge around 15 per cent above standard cost and are available from a number of utility companies.	Easy to convert your home without any modifications.
photovoltaic panels	1			1	3		5	Currently expensive and only produce electricity during daylight hours. Has good potential provided system cost is reduced.	Suitable for southerly facing facades only. Best suited to sunny climates.
wind turbines	1			1	3	1	6	Large scale wind turbines are more efficient.	Expensive. Only suitable in remote locations with wind speeds of 25km/hr or more.
standard utility company	3			3	1		7	These use traditional power stations which are energy intensive and wasteful.	Avoid where possible.
Water conservation									
showers	1	1		1	1	1	5	Showers use only two-fifths of the water used in a bath. Avoid power showers.	

Category	Energy consumption	Durability	Recyclability	Environmental pollution	Installation cost	Maintenance cost	Overall eco-score	Comments	Suitability
			Ecofriendliness						
spray taps	1	1		1	1	1	5	Can be retrofitted to standard taps (which is unattractive) or new spray taps can be fitted when upgrading.	Use in hand basins or in the kitchen.
rainwater collecting system	1	1		1	2	1	6	Collecting rainwater for gardening is easy but collecting for washing and toilets requires significant investment.	
dual flush toilets	2	1		2	1	1	7	These can save at least half of the water used in traditional toilets.	
composting toilets	1	1		1	3	2	8	If you are not connected to the main sewers, it can be cheaper than building a sewage treatment plant.	
grey water recycling systems	1	2		1	3	2	9	Recycling bath water for flushing toilets or for gardening is relatively expensive, but can be justified in new buildings.	
Heating/energy conservation									
boiler controls and thermostats	1	1		1	1	1	5	Choose controls that select hot water separately from heating. Choose internal thermostat and set it to below 20°C. Use a seven day timer clock.	
water tank and pipes	1	1		1	1	1	5	Insulate with thick rockwool jacket and cork pipe insulation.	
loft insulation	1	1		1	1	1	5	200 m of loft insulation is cheap to install and will reduce heat loss considerably.	
floor draught-proofing	1	1		1	1	1	5	Necessary in older homes with timber floors. If possible insulate between floor joists and seal behind skirting boards.	

Category	Energy consumption	Durability	Recyclability	Environmental pollution	Installation cost	Maintenance cost	Overall eco-score	Comments	Suitability
			Ecofriendliness						
window and door draught-proofing	1	1		2	1	1	6	Reduces heating bills in winter. Seal over letter boxes on doors, too.	
curtains	1	2		1	1	1	6	These should be interlined and drawn in the evening.	
condensing gas boiler	1	2		1	2	1	7	If you are upgrading, choose a high efficiency condensing boiler to minimise running costs and pollution.	
secondary glazing	1	1		2	1	2	7	Use glass with low emissivity (low e) film to reduce heat loss even further.	Use if your single glazed windows are in good condition.
timber stove	2	1		1	2	2	8		Only suitable in the country with good local timber.
draught lobbies	2	1		2	2	1	8	If you have the space, lobbies on front and back doors will help to keep heat in and dust out.	
low e double glazing	2	1		1	2	2	8	Only slightly more expensive than traditional glazing. Worth the extra cost.	Good for living rooms and cold or shaded elevations.
wall insulation	2	1		2	2	1	8	Sensible option for cavity walls, particularly in windy and wet locations.	
solar thermal panels and condensing gas boiler	1	2		1	3	2	9	Expensive but environmentally sound improvement to condensing boilers.	Only sensible to install solar thermal panels once you have undertaken other improvements to your home.

Useful contact details

Updates and more detailed information is available on ecofriendlyhome.com
For any queries please email on info@ecofriendlyhome.com

Eco-organisations

Friends of the Earth
Environmental charity
Nationwide 020 7490 1555
www.foe.co.uk

FSC (Forest Stewardship Council)
International organisation promoting sustainable forest management
Powys 01686 413916

Greenpeace
Environmental charity
Nationwide 020 7865 8100
www.greenpeace.org.uk

Soil Association
Supports organic farming
Bristol 01453 752985
www.soilassociation.org

Soil Association (Woodmark)
Operates an FSC approved woodland management programme
Avon 01179 290661
www.soilassociation.org

TRADA (Timber Research and Development Agency)
Independent research on timbers
Buckinghamshire 01494 563091
www.trada.co.uk

World Wide Fund for Nature
International charity supporting nature and the environment
Surrey 01483 426444
www.wwf-uk.org

Eco-design

Association for Environmentally Conscious Building
Promotes green building and has an extensive list of green suppliers and designers
Camarthenshire 01559 370908
www.aecb.net

Centre for Alternative Technology
Information on ecological design
Powys 01654 702400
www.cat.org.uk

Ecological Design Association
Promotes eco-home design
Gloucestershire 01453 765575
www.mcc.ac.uk/eda

Parnham Trust
Promotes the craft of sustainable wood management, carpentry and furniture design
Dorset 01308 862204
www.hookepark.com

RIBA (Royal Institute of British Architects)
Information on mainstream and specialist architects
London 020 7580 5533
www.architecture.com

Walter Segal Self-Build Trust
Advice on building your own home using the Walter Segal method
London 01668 213544
wssbt@powernet.co.uk

Renewable energy companies

Green Electron
Nationwide 0345 419484
www.greenelectron.co.uk
Solar Century
Promotes solar energy
Nationwide 020 8332 6565
www.solarcentury.co.uk

Unit(e)
Nationwide 01249 705550
www.unit-energy.co.uk

Recycling organisations

Architectural Salvage Index
Information on reusing building products, including a list of salvage dealers
Surrey 01483 203221
www.handr.co.uk

Salvo
Provides advice on reusing building products, including a list of architectural salvage dealers
Northumberland 01890 820333
www.salvo.co.uk

Wastewatch
Advice on recycling, including a guide to buying recycled products
Nationwide 0870 243 0136
www.wastewatch.org.uk

Government and trade associations

Energy Efficiency Council
Draught control and insulation
advice and information
Surrey 01428 654011
theceed@compuserve.com

Energy Saving Trust
Provides grants and advice on energy
saving measures at home
Nationwide 0345 277200
www.est.org.uk

Ethical Consumer Research
Association
Publishes ethical consumer
magazines
Manchester 0161 226 2929
www.ethicalconsumer.org

Fair Trade Foundation
Promotes fair trade
London 020 7405 5942
www.fairtrade.org.uk

National Energy Foundation
Free renewable energy advice
Milton Keynes 0800 138 0889
www.natenergy.co.uk/renewables.html

Solar Trade Association
Advice on solar heating
Cornwall 01208 873518

UK Ecolabelling
Information on environmentally
sound products
London 020 7890 6567
www.europa.eu.int/ecolabel

General eco-merchants

B&Q
A mainstream DIY store with good
eco-credentials on many UK lines
www.diy.co.uk

Construction Resource Centre
Sells a wide range of eco-products
and also gives building and design
advice
London 020 7450 2211
www.ecoconstruct.com

Environmental Construction Products
Sells and advises on conservatories
and other green building products
West Yorkshire 01484 854898
www.ecoproducts.co.uk

Green Guide
Regional updated guide to
purchasing green products
London 020 7354 2709
www.greenguide.co.uk

The Green Shop
Sells green products
Stroud 01452 770629
www.greenshop.co.uk

Traidcraft Exchange
Organisation supporting fair trade
Nationwide 0191 491 0591
www.traidcraft.co.uk

Other useful contacts

Green Futures Magazine
Promotes sustainable futures
Cambridge 01223 568017

Ethical-junction
An online directory of ethical
business
www.ethical-junction. org

National Pure Water Association
Campaigns for safe water
Wakefield 01924 254433
www.npwa.freeserve.co.uk

Henry Doubleday Research
Association
Provides organic research and advice
01203 303517
www.hdra.org.uk

Index

A

acrylic 81
air 29
    filtering 29
air-conditioning 25, 43, 45
allergies 62, 152–3
aluminium 12, 53, 70, 76, 103
ammonia 36
appliances
    household 34
    kitchen 103
argon gas 39
asphalt 14
attic 22, 71, 132
awning 44

B

babies 138–41
bamboo 63, 117
banister 87
basement 22, 130
basin 119
bathrooms 20, 21, 55, 58, 114–19
beanbag 94, 146
bedrooms 20, 21, 22, 48, 108–13
    linen 113
bedsit 128–9
bidet 117
bikes 126, 145
blinds 26, 90, 132, 135
boiler 25, 38, 160
    condensing 41
brass 12
brick 60
bulk buying 12
bunkbed 143

C

candles 36, 122
carpets 9, 20, 31, 55, 58, 60, 62, 152
    cleaning 162
cars 10, 12, 126, 149
ceramic 59
chairs 149
    dining 107
    high chair 141
children 142–5
chimney 41
chlorine 34, 36
chrome 12
clay 14
cleaning 164–7
coir 29, 62, 110
colours 26, 46, 48–9
community 8, 9, 10–11, 18
composting 169
computers 124, 126–7, 144
concrete 14, 58
conservatory 18, 90, 134–5
cookers 102
cooking 101
copper 70, 76, 117
Corbusier 108
cork 68
corridor 86
cotton 62, 80
council 10, 29
curtains 26, 39, 110, 111
cutlery 77

D

damp 31, 55, 158
damp proofing 32, 130
daybed 95
desk 126
detergents 34, 166–7
diesel 11

dining rooms 21, 22, 104–7
disability 149
dishes 34
dishwashers 34, 166
doors 73
    French 90
    mat 29
    stopper 38
downlighters 27
downpipes 157
downsizing 148
drains 19, 31, 36, 156
draughts 40
    exclusion tape 18, 130
dry cleaning 166
Dunster, Bill 13
duvet 80, 113
dye
    natural 46
    synthetic 47, 66

E

eco-labelling 34
ecology 8
eco-warriors 9
electricity 12, 158
energy
    renewable 12
    saving 101
Energy Star compatible 34, 126
entranceway 86–9
ethanol 11
extensions 22
extract fans 114, 123
extractor hoods 102

F

fabrics 80–3
fan
  ceiling 44
feather 83
filters, carbon 34
filter systems
  reed bed 36
  tap bases 34
fire
  electric 37
  gas, 29, 30
  wood 29, 37
fireplaces 95
fittings 74–83
flashing 32
flats 22
flax 83
floors
  bathroom 121
  cleaning 161
  coverings 56–64
  parquet 57
  subfloor 54
  wood 9, 150
flues 30
fluorine 34
food 99
forests 75
fridges 12
friendliness 8
Froebel, Friedrich 144
fuels, fossil 12
  smokeless 30
  smoky 30
fun 9
furniture 12, 52, 74, 147
  bathroom 114–23
  metal 75
  monolithic 14
  portable 53

second-hand 12
studio 128–9
wood 74
futon 74, 109, 146, 147

G

garage 22, 148
gardens 14, 15, 24, 36, 41, 134, 156
gas 160
glass
  bricks 70
  recycled 74, 78
glazing 38
  double 19
  single 19
granite 100
gravel 52
gutter 157

H

halls 21, 26
heat recovery system 40
heating 37–42
  bills 40
  electric 27
  gas 9, 19
  solar 42
  wood-fired 19
hemp 63
herbs 14, 30, 123, 153
hessian 68, 83, 92
Hope house 13
hypoallergenic 58, 153

I

ionisers 31
incense 36
insulation 37, 55, 69, 71, 159
iron 77

J

jute 62, 63, 64

K

kitchens 20, 21, 22, 55, 70, 76, 96–101
  cleaning 164–7
  kilims 62
  special needs 149
  triangle 58
  utensils 139

L

landfills 14
lead 77
  flashings 34
leather 52, 81, 83
legionnaire's disease 34
lighting 25–28
  artificial 25
  backlighting 105
  bathroom 122
  bedroom 26, 110
  choosing 25–28
  desk 26, 27, 126
  dimmer switch 138
  effective 102
  electric 26
  fluorescent 9, 26, 28
  halogen 28
  low-energy bulbs 18
  natural 20, 25, 28
  spotlights 118
  tungsten 27, 28
  wall washers 28
light pipes 26
lignin paste 64
limescale 159
linoleum 64

living rooms 20, 21, 48, 90–5
loft 38
low e (emissivity) glazing 38, 73, 121

M

materials 52–53
    ecofriendly 52
    heavy 58
    options 90
    toxic 32, 53
mattresses 109
    pads 113
metal 52, 70, 75
    recycled 74
    utensils 76
mezzanine 125
micro fuel cells 11
microwave 128
minimalism 90, 96
mirror 129
mood 48
mosquitoes 170
moths 170
multifunctional 9
Murcatt, Glen 73
Musil, Robert 17
muslin 45, 90

N

nappies 140
noise 18, 108
nursery 138–9
nylon 81

O

oil 52
overshadowing 19, 20, 21, 42

P

paints 32, 158
    casein 68
    distemper 68
    ecofriendly 66
    synthetic 67
paper
    lanterns 90
    recycled 14, 126
parks 10
patterns 46
    fractal 49
    natural 48, 49
pergola 43, 44
photovoltaic systems 11
pipework 33, 34, 35, 159
plants 14, 15, 22, 41, 43, 123, 153, 160
plaster 65
plastic 78
    bags 13, 53
playrooms 22, 65
plumbing 20, 31, 114, 159
pollution 8, 12, 18, 19, 20, 21, 31
    mineral 68
polyester 81
pond 36, 156
pots and pans 103
power stations 11, 12, 28
PVC (polyvinyl chloride) 64

R

radiators 39, 42
radon 19, 30
raffia 68
rainwater 33, 36
    butts 33
recycling 9, 12, 20, 28, 56
roof 44, 71
    asbestos 34

insulation 38
    metal 72
    thatch 71
    turf covering 71
    zinc 34
rubber 64
rugs 49, 54, 58, 60, 127
    cleaning 163

S

salvage yards 60, 117
sand 29, 52
seagrass 62, 63
sea shells 29
seasons 9, 14
secondhand 11
security 45
Seigal, Walter 24
self-build 24
shading 44, 135
shadow 27
Shaker style 98
shaving 120
shelves 127, 132
    bracket 89
    carousel 99
    fixed 93
shoe rack 29
shower 118
shutters 43
silk 62, 82
sisal 62, 63
skylights 26
slate 32
soap 120
sofa 92
solar panels 37, 38, 42
space 22, 46
spotlights 27
staircases 26, 87, 125, 149
steel 77

stone 52, 59
storage 88, 92, 99, 110, 128, 140,
  143
stove
    wood burning 41
studio 128
study 88, 105, 124
subsidence 157
sunroom 22
sunshine 11, 42
surveyor 18, 31

T

table-cloth 104
table linen 106
Tanizaki 27
tatami mats 61
tencel 82
terrace 72
terrazzo 14, 58, 59
texture 48–9
thermostat 38, 41
tiles 32, 69
    clay 71
    concrete 71
    cork 69
    glazed 72
    rubber 70
    slate 71
    splash-back 100
timber 56
toilets 119
towels 123
toys 140, 142, 144
transport 10
trees 41, 157
trickle vents 31, 32

U

upholstery 83, 106
uplights 27
utility rooms 21

V

van der Rohe, Mies 11
varnishes 57, 67
ventilation 12, 30, 31
    heat recovery system 30, 153
    passive stack 102, 123
    positive extract system 31
verandah 21, 22, 45
views 22
vines 44
vinyl 64
viscose 82
VOC (volatile organic compounds) 67

W

wallpaper 49, 68, 69
walls 39
    cleaning 163
    external 73, 158
    insulation 66
    loadbearing 65
    solid 65
    studwork 65, 66
washing
    clothes 167
    dishes 34
waste 8,12, 100, 168–9
water
    conserving 35, 166
    grey 36
    recycled 33
    tap 36
water pipes 19, 35, 54
water tank 19, 33, 34, 35

waxes 57, 67, 81, 161
wicker 92
windows 38, 72
    bathroom 121
    bedroom 113
    French 156
wind turbines 11, 12
wiring 20
wood 14, 53, 57
    panelling 69
wool 62, 80, 151
workshop 22
wormeries 169
Wright, Frank Lloyd 85

Z

zinc 78

Picture credits

t= top, l=left, r=right, b=bottom, c= centre, cb=centre below, ca=centre above, mp=main picture. EWA=www.elizabethwhiting.com

2/3 IKEA; 4 The Holding Company; 5t Bhs:
5c Christy; 5b Bhs; 6mp Dave Young; 6bl
Elgin & Hall Ltd; 6bc General Electric
Mazda; 6br Solar Century; 8/9 Ed
Reeve/Living Etc/IPC Syndication; 9 Elgin &
Hall Ltd; 10 Gettyone Stone; 11t Solar
Century; 11b Images Colour Library;   13
Dave Young; 14t STOKKE FABRIKKER AS;
14c Elgin & Hall Ltd; 14b General Electric
Mazda; 15t David Murray; 15b Image Bank;
16mp The Timber Decking Association; 16bl
The Velux Company Ltd; 16bc English
Hurdle; 16br Prêt à Vivre; 18 Jeremy
Cockayne/Arcaid; 19t Cuprinol; 19c
International; 19b Laura Ashley; 20/21
NEXT Home; 21 English Hurdle; 22 Laura
Ashley; 23 The Velux Company Ltd; 24 Paul
Smoothy; 25 Simon Kenny /Belle/Arcaid; 27
Chris Gascoigne/View; 28t General Electric
Mazda; 28c Jam; 28b Ocean; 29 Jon
Boucher/ EWA; 30 Nolte; 32 Neil
Lorimer/EWA; 33t The Timber Decking
Association; 33b Rodney Hyett/EWA; 34
Gettyone Stone; 35 David Murray; 36
Homebase; 37 Elgin & Hall Ltd; 39t Prêt à
Vivre; 39b Klóber UK; 41 Austroflamm; 42
Tommy Candler/ EWA; 43l Peter
Woloszynski/ EWA; 43r Neil Lorimer/EWA;
44 Rodney Hyett/ EWA; 45l Nedra
Westwater/EWA; 45r Sake Powell/EWA;
46/47 Rodney Hyett/EWA; 47
International; 48tl Prêt à Vivre; 48tr
Monkwell; 48ca International; 48cb Bhs;
48b Swish; 49t House; 49b Crown Paint;
50mp LASSCO Flooring; 50bl Kersaint
Cobb; 50bc Auro Organic Paint Supplies;
50br Descamps; 52t The Holding Company;
52bl Magnet; 52br Stone Age; 53 LASSCO
Flooring; 54/55 James Morris/Axiom; 56
LASSCO Flooring; 57 Natural Flooring
Direct; 58tl Roger Oates Design; 58tr
Roundel Design; 58bl Resin Building
Products Ltd; 58br McCord; 59
Bartholomew Conservatories; 60 The Rug
Company; 61t Image Bank; 61b Jim
Holmes/Axiom; 62t Kersaint Cobb; 62ca
Natural Flooring Direct; 62cb,b Kersaint
Cobb; 63 Kersaint Cobb; 64 Forbo-Nairn
Ltd; 65 Kersaint Cobb; 67 Auro Organic
Paint Supplies; 68 Crown Wallcoverings &
Home Furnishings; 69tl Stone Age; 69tr
McCord; 69bl Fired Earth; 69br Ariston; 70l
LASSCO Flooring; 70r Dalsouple; 71 Graham
Henderson/EWA; 72 Armitage Shanks; 73
Jim Holmes/Arcaid; 74 Futon Company;
74/75t Sanderson; 74/75b Magnet; 76t
Shaker; 76ca,cb House; 76b Lakeland
Limited; 78 Peter Cook/View; 79 Habitat;
80/81t Descamps; 80/81b Earth Tones
Collection; 81t Earth Tones Collection; 81b
House of Fraser; 82 Sanderson; 83 McCord;
84mp Vale Garden Houses Ltd; 84bl Marks
& Spencer Direct; 84bc Nolte; 84br Crown
Paint; 86t LimeStone Gallery; 87l Chris
Gascoigne/View; 87r Dennis Gilbert/View;
88t The Holding Company; 88b Elgin & Hall
Ltd; 89 Chris Drake/Living Etc/IPC
Syndication; 90 Ligne Roset; 90/1 Peter
Aprahamian/Living Etc/IPC Syndication;
92tl The Holding Company; 92tr Marks &
Spencer Direct; 92b Elgin & Hall Ltd; 93t
Cuprinol; 93b Wilman Interiors; 94 Elgin &
Hall Ltd; 95 Sanderson; 96t Ariston; 96b
Nolte; 96/97 Dennis Gilbert/View; 98
Shaker; 99t The Holding Company;
99bl,bc,br Magnet; 100 Magnet; 101
Stonell Ltd; 102 Peter Cook/View; 103t,c,b
Neff; 103r Marks & Spencer Direct; 104t
IKEA; 104b Elgin & Hall Ltd; 104/105 Peter
Cook/View; 105 Marks & Spencer Direct;
106 Magnet; 107tl Bhs; 108t Yves
Delorme; 108/109 Dennis Gilbert/View;
109t Marks & Spencer Direct; 109b Futon
Company; 110l Sanderson; 110r Futon
Company; 110/111 James Morris/Axiom;
112 Elgin & Hall Ltd; 113t Marks & Spencer
Direct; 113b Found; 114t Colourwash; 114b
Crown Paint; 114/115 Chris
Gascoigne/View; 116 Armitage Shanks;
117tl Magnet; 117tr House; 117bl LASSCO
R.B.K; 117br Marks & Spencer Direct; 118l
Dennis Gilbert/View; 118r Marks & Spencer
Direct; 119tl Magnet; 119bl G.E.C.
Anderson; 119br Armitage Shanks; 120l
Found; 120r Christy; 121tl Dalsouple;
121tr International; 121bl LimeStone
Gallery; 121br Armitage Shanks; 122t Wax
Lyrical; 122b Premium/Arcaid; 123 Ocean;
124 Elgin & Hall Ltd; 124/125 Ed
Reeve/Living Etc/IPC Syndication; 125br
JELD-WEN UK; 126t,c Ocean; 126b Found;
127 Elgin & Hall Ltd; 128t IKEA; 128b
Neff; 129 Forbo-Nairn Ltd; 130t Julie
Phipps/Arcaid; 130b Premium/Arcaid;
130/131 Julie Phipps/Arcaid; 132 The Velux
Company Ltd; 132/133 Dennis
Gilbert/View; 134t Vale Garden Houses Ltd;
134b Bartholomew Conservatories;
134/135,135 Vale Garden Houses Ltd;
136mp Gettyone Stone; 136bl,br The Stock
Market UK; 136bc IKEA; 138 Gettyone
Stone; 139t,c Construction Resources;
139b Elgin & Hall Ltd; 140t IKEA;
140bl,bc,br Found; 141 STOKKE FABRIKKER
AS; 142 Telegraph Colour Library; 143t The
Velux Company Ltd; 143b Boots; 144 The
Stock Market UK; 145t Ocean; 145b
Gettyone Stone; 146 Gettyone Stone; 147
The Stock Market UK; 148 Images Colour
Library; 149t JELD-WEN UK; 149b smart
car; 150 Gettyone Stone; 151t Karl-
Dietrich Buhler/EWA; 151b The Stock
Market UK; 152/153 Image Bank; 153
Grand Illusions; 154bl,bc David Murray;
156 Image Bank; 159 David Murray; 160
David Murray; 162t Dyson; 162b Gettyone
Stone; 163 Kersaint Cobb; 164 David
Murray; 165c House of Fraser; 166 Image
Bank; 168/169t Gettyone Stone; 168/169b
Telegraph Colour Library; 170 IKEA.

Suppliers and acknowledgements

Suppliers

Carroll & Brown would particularly like to thank the following companies for supplying invaluable information and images:

Ariston
08700 104305

Armitage Shanks
0800 866966
www.armitage-shanks.co.uk

Auro Organic Paint Supplies
01799 584888
www.auroorganic.co.uk

Austroflamm
01392 474060
austro@stovax.com

Bartholomew
01428 658771
www.bartholomewconservatories.co.uk

Bhs
020 7262 3288

Boots
0845 0708090
www.boots.co.uk

Christy
0345 585252

Colourwash
020 8459 8918
www.colourwash.co.uk

Construction Resources
020 7450 2211
www.ecoconstruct.com

Crown Paint
01254 704951
www.crownpaint.co.uk

Crown Wallcoverings & Home Furnishings
0800 4581544
www.crown-wallcoverings.co.uk

Cuprinol
01373 475000

Dalsouple
01984 667551

Descamps
020 7235 6957
www.descamps.com

Dyson
01666 827200
www.dyson.com

Earth Tones Collection
020 8354 0333
www.earthtones.co.uk

Elgin & Hall Ltd
Customer helpline 01677 450100
www.elgin.co.uk

English Hurdle
01823 698418
www.hurdle.co.uk

Fired Earth
01295 814300
www.firedearth.co.uk

Forbo-Nairn Ltd
01592 643777
www.marmoleum.co.uk

Found
0800 3168121
www.foundat.co.uk

Futon Company
0845 6094455
www.futoncompany.co.uk

G.E.C. Anderson
01442 826999
www.gecanderson.co.uk

General Electric Mazda
020 8626 8500

Grand Illusions
01747 854092

Habitat
0845 6010740
www.habitat.net

The Holding Company
020 7610 0160
www.theholdingcompany.co.uk

Homebase
0645 801800
www.homebase.co.uk

House
01725 552549
www.housemailorder.co.uk

House of Fraser
020 7963 2236
www.houseoffraser.co.uk

IKEA
020 8208 5607
www.ikea.com

International
01962 717001/2
www.plascon.co.uk

Jam
020 7278 5567
www.jamdesign.co.uk

JELD-WEN UK
0870 1260000
www.jeld-wen.co.uk

Kersaint Cobb
01675 430430

Klóber Limited
01934 853224

Lakeland Limited
01539 488100
www.lakelandlimited.com

LASSCO Flooring/
LASSCO R.B.K
020 7749 9944
www.lassco.co.uk

Laura Ashley
0870 5622116
www.lauraashley.com

Ligne Roset
0845 6020267
www.ligne-roset.co.uk

LimeStone Gallery
020 7735 8555

Magnet
Stockist information 0800 192192

Marks & Spencer Direct
020 7268 1234
www.marks-and-spencer.co.uk

McCord
0870 9087005
www.mccord.uk.com

Monkwell
01202 752944
www.monkwell.com

Natural Flooring Direct
0800 454721
www.reeveflooring.co.uk

Neff
Stockist information 08705 133090
www.neff.co.uk

NEXT Home
0845 6007000
www.next.co.uk

Nolte
01279 868500
www.nolte-kuchen.de

Ocean
0870 2426283
www.oceancatalogue.com

Prêt à Vivre
020 8960 6111
www.pretavivre.com

Resin Building Products Ltd
01302 881394
www.webadsuk.co.uk

Roger Oates Design
01531 631611
www.rogeroates.com

Roundel Design
01580 712666

Sanderson
01895 201509
www.sanderson-uk.com

Shaker
020 7935 9461
www.shaker.co.uk

smart car
www.smart.com

Solar Century
0870 735 8100
www.solarcentury.co.uk

STOKKE FABRIKKER AS, Norway
www.stokke.com

Stone Age
020 7385 7954

Stonell Ltd
01892 833500

Swish
01827 64242

The Timber Decking Association
01977 679812
www.tda.org.uk

Vale Garden Houses Ltd
01476 564433

The Velux Company Ltd
0800 3168820
www.velux.co.uk

Wax Lyrical
020 8561 0235

Wilman Interiors
0800 581984

Yves Delorme
01296 610212
www.yvesdelorme.com

Acknowledgements

Project Editor Madeleine Jennings
Designer Vimit Punater

Deputy Art Director Tracy Timson

Photographers Jules Selmes, David Murray

IT management Elisa Merino, Paul Stradling
Production manager Karol Davies

Picture researchers Clare Carter, Sandra
Schneider, Richard Soar
Proofreader Clare Hacking
Index Madeleine Jennings

Thanks also to Simon Daley for original
design and Vimit Punater for technical
illustrations

Author acknowledgements

Thanks to all my friends and family for
putting up with my passion, my work
colleagues for helping me organise my life
when time was tight, my old friend Rachel
Aris who commissioned this book, and my
editor Madeleine Jennings for her advice,
patience and friendly bonhomie.